OXFORD
SCIENCE 1
programme A-D

Consultant Editor: **Paul Denley**

Managing Editor: **Stephen Pople**

Steering Committee:

Keith Bishop
Peter Ellis
Phil Lidstone
David Lossl
Jim Sage
Linda Scott
Susan Williams

Additional Authors:

Terry Hudson
Barry Penn
Mark Williams

Oxford University Press

Contents

Module B
Microbes and health

Key
YI Your ideas
LF Looking further
UNI Using new ideas

Module C
Materials and mixtures

Module D
Living with electricity

Key

YI	Your ideas
LF	Looking further
UNI	Using new ideas

Introduction

This book is just one part of the Oxford Science Programme. Its investigations and activities have been specially designed for Key Stage 3 of the National Curriculum for Science. The book is divided into four modules, each dealing with a different aspect of science:

Module A
Looking at life

The Earth is home for many types of plants and animals. They all have their own special features and places to live. In this module, you investigate some small animals and plants and their living places. You look at the effects of seasonal and daily changes, the way humans control their own living conditions and how other forms of life can be affected. You investigate how animals and plants can vary from one to another. You look at the ways in which living things on Earth can be grouped by their different features.

Module B
Microbes and health

Microbes are tiny, living things and can only be seen with a microscope. They are all around you, in the air, in foods and in the garden. Some do a useful job while others are harmful to us. In this module, you investigate how some microbes make new foods, while others make old foods rot. You find out how some microbes produce 'goodness' for the garden, while others cause illness and disease. Finally, you look at other things which may help or harm your health.

Module C
Materials and mixtures

In this module, you start by looking at different materials, how they behave, and what they are used for. You have to design tests to find out which materials are most suitable for different jobs. You look into solids, liquids and gases, how they can be measured and how some dissolve in others. You investigate mixtures of materials, the different ways of separating them and why we so often need to unmix things.

Module D
Living with electricity

Electricity can appear when you rub things. It can do useful jobs when you let it flow from a battery. It can even light up the sky in a flash. In this module you start by investigating materials which produce electricity when rubbed. Next you look at 'portable' electricity from a battery, how circuits are wired to use electricity, and how electricity can be used safely. Then you investigate magnets, magnetic forces and how electricity can make magnetism.

Each module is made up of double-page spreads, but these have been grouped in a special way. We've called each group of spreads a unit. At the start of each unit, you will be asked to think about *your* ideas and to share and discuss them with others. Next, you will carry out some investigations to test your ideas. Finally, you will have the chance to use any new ideas you have learned. So, as you work through the spreads in each unit, the pattern will be:

> your ideas
> looking further
> using new ideas

The last spread in each module is called *Stepping stones*. It will present you with new challenges covering the whole module.

Start investigating and see what you can find out!

OXFORD
SCIENCE
programme

A Looking at life

Follow the rabbit

A rabbit is finding her way across the countryside in the big picture. She starts at the top of the hill and ends up by the dandelion in the corner.

1 Write a story about the rabbit's journey. Include in your story as many of the plants and animals in the picture as you can. Don't forget that the rabbit will need to eat and drink on her way, and that other animals may try to eat her.

Plants and animals

There are lots of different plants and animals in the big picture. With your group:

2 List all the different types of plants you can see.

3 List all the different types of animals you can see. (Remember, an animal is any living thing that is not a plant!)

4 **Classify** (sort out) your animals into two groups, those that fly and those that don't.

5 Now classify your animals into three groups. You can choose the groups yourself this time.

6 Make a poster of your groups so that the rest of the class can see them. How many ways of classifying have the class produced?

7 Choose one animal from your list of animals.
   Where do you think it would shelter?
   Where do you think it would find food?
   What other animals do you think it would have to hide from?

Humans sometimes do things which change the way in which animals and plants can live and grow.

8 What examples can you think of? The big picture might help you.

Habitats

The area in which an animal or plant lives is called its **habitat**. For example, the pond in the big picture is a habitat for newts. Different animals and plants have different habitats. Three examples of habitats not in the picture are jungle, pasture and the sea.

9 What different habitats can you see in the big picture?

Newts in their habitat

10 Choose one of the habitats in the big picture.
   What plants would you find in the habitat?
   What animals would you find in the habitat?
   How would you expect the light to vary in the habitat?
   How would you expect the temperature to vary in the habitat?

Somewhere to live

Investigate

Find out where the animals in the pictures like to live and what conditions they prefer.

Things to think about
- In what places will you need to look for the animals?
- What information will you need to record about each place? For example, should you record the conditions – such as whether the place is damp or dry, light or dark, and what types of plants are around?
- How will you record your results?

What to do
- Plan your investigation.
- List the places in the school which you would like to survey.
- Check your plans with your teacher.
- Collect the information you need. **Remember: all living things should be handled gently.**
- Make a poster to present your information.

Food and shelter

Investigate

Find out what types of food and shelter are used by the animals in the pictures.

Things to think about
- Will you look to see what food and shelter the animals normally have?
- Will you put different foods outside, then come back later to see which ones have been eaten?
- Will you bring some of the animals into the laboratory and give them different foods and shelters?
- How will you record your results?

What to do
- Plan your investigation.
- Ask your teacher to check your plan.
- Collect the information you need.
- Make an information leaflet for primary school pupils called 'Food and shelter'. Draw the animals you have studied and give as much information as you can about their food and shelter. You could use **reference books**, like encyclopedias, to find extra information.

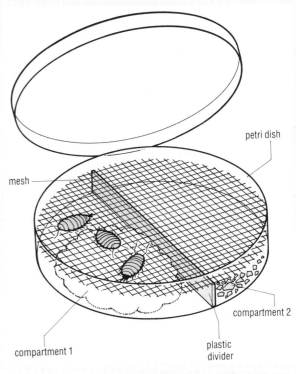

mesh

petri dish

compartment 1

plastic divider

compartment 2

Choice chamber

A choice for woodlice

You can use a **choice chamber** to find out what conditions tiny animals prefer. A choice chamber has two compartments. Tiny animals can walk on the mesh above either compartment. You can put different materials in the two compartments to make the conditions different in each.

Investigate

Find out whether woodlice prefer damp or dry conditions.

You need
Woodlice, choice chamber, silica gel crystals, cotton wool, water, pipette, beaker.

Useful information
Silica gel is a chemical which absorbs moisture from the air. For it to work, it must be kept dry until it is needed. You can use it to make the air dry inside a container.

Things to think about
- How are you going to make one side of the choice chamber damp and the other dry?
- How many woodlice will you put in the choice chamber?

- How will you be able to tell which conditions the woodlice prefer?
- How many times will you count the way the woodlice spread out in the choice chamber?
- Will you need to use a clock or stopwatch to time any part of your investigation?
- How will you record your results?

What to do
- Plan your investigation.
- Ask your teacher to check your plan.
- Carry out your investigation.
- Present your results using a chart.
- What do your results tell you about the conditions woodlice prefer?
- Did other groups in your class find the same as you? Give reasons for any differences you find.

Each of the photographs shows a different habitat.

1 Choose one of the habitats. Describe the conditions in this habitat using the following words:

light   *decaying leaves*

shade   *insect life*

damp soil   *plant life*

dry soil   *water*

Try to find out the names of the plants in the photo. Your teacher may have books to help you.

2 Look at the other three habitats. For each one, describe the conditions and try to find out the names of the plants.

Different types of plant grow in each habitat:

3 Why do you think this is so? Your descriptions may give you some clues.

4 Study each picture. Which one shows the most types of plant?

5 Put the pictures in order, with the one showing the most plant types first.

6 Why do you think some habitats have more types of plant growing in them than others?

Habitats for plants

Investigate

Find out whether different plants in the school grounds prefer different habitats.

You need
Books to help you identify types of plants.

What to do

- Choose three areas of the school grounds that are different habitats for plants. Make a sketch map to show the places you have chosen.
- Make a list of the conditions in each habitat. For example: damp soil, lots of insects, wall.
- List as many plants as possible in each habitat. Use reference books to help you name them.
- Choose one plant you have investigated. List the conditions it seems to prefer.
- Choose other plants and list the conditions they seem to prefer.
- Make a poster showing the conditions preferred by each of the plants you have chosen. Compare your results with those of other groups.

Growing problems

Look at the picture with the tractor in it and answer these with your group:.

7 What job is being done by the tractor in the picture?

8 Why is this being done?

9 What would happen to the plants if no treatment was given?

10 What problems could this treatment cause?

Look at this picture from Brazil of the tree being cut down and answer these:

11 How long do you think it will take for a new tree to grow?

12 List some uses of wood.

13 What materials can people use instead of wood?

14 What do you think is meant by **recycling**? Why does it help to save trees?

A dispute on the farm

Mrs Muir keeps free range hens for their eggs. A few days ago, Mrs Muir developed a skin rash. Around the same time, her hens stopped laying and some of her garden flowers died. Mrs Muir's house is next to a field of wheat owned by Mr Lacey, who is a farmer. About a week ago, on a rather windy day, he sprayed his wheat with insecticides.

15 What do you think **insecticides** are?

16 Imagine you are Mrs Muir. Write a letter to your local newspaper explaining what has happened. Say what you think has caused your problems.

17 Mr Lacey did not always use insecticides on his crops. Look at the information in the table. In what year do you think he started using insecticides?

18 Imagine you are Mr Lacey. Write a letter to the newspaper explaining why you use insecticides on your crop. Put some figures into your letter to try and convince the readers how important insecticides are.

19 In your group, decide who has written the most convincing letter, Mrs Muir or Mr Lacey.

20 Present the information in the yield table in a more interesting way. You could draw a graph or a chart. In a chart you could use a picture symbol for each tonne.

21 Work out the average yield of wheat per year before and after Mr Lacey started using insecticides.

Year	Yield in tonnes
1	4.5
2	5.0
3	4.0
4	3.5
5	4.0
6	7.0
7	8.0
8	7.5
9	8.0
10	8.0

We sometimes divide the year into four **seasons**. With your group:

1 Make a chart with four columns. Write the name of a different season at the head of each column. Put one feature of each season into each column. For example, in winter it is *cold*. Go on filling up the columns until you run out of ideas.

Look at the pictures of the trees.

2 Which season is each of the pictures showing?

3 Put the pictures in their correct order, starting with spring.

A

B

C

D

Look at the pictures of how a butterfly develops.

4 List the pictures in their correct order, starting with the **egg** stage.

5 At what times of the year are you most likely to see each stage?

6 What do you think might happen to the adults in winter?

7 Find out what the butterfly feeds on at each stage.

a

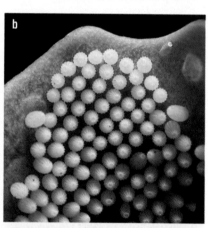

b

c

d

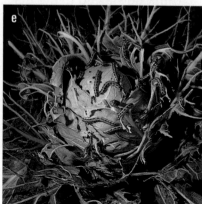

e

Your daily cycle

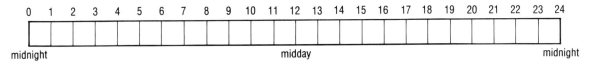

A **cycle** is something that happens over and over again. Each day is a cycle.

8 Copy the chart. On your chart, shade or colour in the time you spend each day: eating, sleeping, watching TV, exercising, doing something else. Make a key to show what each shade or colour means.

9 Add up the total number of hours you spend on each activity. (Work it out to the nearest hour.)

10 Make a bar chart showing the amount of time you spend on each activity.

11 Describe the things in your daily cycle that help you:
keep fit
keep healthy
keep your mind alert and active.

12 Describe the things in your daily cycle that *stop* you keeping fit, healthy and alert.

Julie's problem page

Julie writes an advice column in a magazine. She has received letters from three people with problems. Look at the letters and the daily cycles of the people who wrote them below.

13 With your group, decide which cycle belongs to each person. Give reasons for each choice.

14 Imagine that you are Julie. Write a brief letter to each person saying what you think is causing their problem and what they should do about it.

Dear Julie,

I am 12 years old and keep on running out of energy. I can't even get enthusiastic about going to discos. I'm easily annoyed, and my mum yells at me all the time. Can you help?

Yours sincerely,
Sam.

Dear Julie,

I like to play hockey, but no one ever seems to want me in their team. Is there something wrong with me? I get out of breath easily, and I can't run as fast as some of the other kids, but if only they would give me a chance! What do you suggest, Julie?

Yours sincerely,
Nicky.

Dear Julie,

I would like your advice. I find it hard to concentrate in class. My marks are getting worse because of this. I would very much like to do better. I know that I'm overweight – do you think this has anything to do with my problem?

Yours sincerely
Chris.

Chart A   Who is it?

Chart B   Who is it?

Chart C   Who is it?

key:

sleeping

exercise

eating

TV

other

A1.5   No place like home

We humans all have a habitat of our own. Often, our habitat is a house and the area around it. Here are fifteen descriptions for you to choose from:

A   Lots of birds
B   Many fields around
C   Lots of traffic
D   Stream or river nearby
E   Lots of litter on the streets
F   Lots of trees growing around
G   Surrounding area very flat
H   An estate of houses around
I   Sea nearby
J   Hills or mountains nearby
K   Factories or industry nearby
L   Good play facilities around for children
M   Snow around for most of the winter
N   School too far away to walk
O   An area where teenagers feel safe walking on their own.

1 Choose the descriptions that suit your own habitat.

2 Choose the descriptions that fit the desert island in the picture.

3 Choose *any five* descriptions. Draw a picture using all of these descriptions.

4 Choose a place on a map of the world. Which of the descriptions would apply to the place you have chosen? What descriptions of your own would you add to the list? Design a poster to give tourists some information about your chosen area.

Controlling human habitats

The pictures show some ways in which people can affect or control their habitats. Answer these with your group.

5 There are lots of ways in which people can get **shelter, food,** and **warmth**. List as many of them as you can.

6 There are many types of **pollution**. Give some examples of pollution from the following:

> *gases   chemicals   oil   radiation   noise   litter*

What do you think people mean by **visual pollution**?

7 What things can people not control in their habitats? (For some clues, think of natural disasters and their causes.)

8 Collect magazine pictures which show people controlling their habitats. Describe each one. Make a poster to display your pictures.

Faraway Places

For each of the pictures, there is some **data** (information) about rainfall and about temperature. You have to decide which picture goes with which data.

9 Copy the rainfall chart. It may help to use graph paper.

10 Draw a second chart using the other set of rainfall information.

11 Decide which chart matches up with each picture.

12 Copy the temperature graph on graph paper.

13 Draw a second graph on graph paper using the other set of temperature information.

14 Decide which graph matches up with each picture.

15 Describe the sort of houses that people living in each place might need.

16 Describe the problems that people living in each of the places might face.

17 Work out the average monthly rainfall for each place.

18 Work out the average monthly temperature for each place.

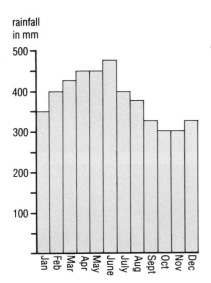

Data A: which place is this?

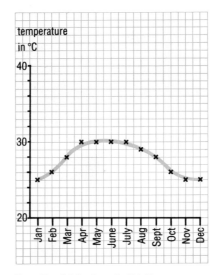

Data B: which place is this?

Month	Rainfall in mm
Jan	30
Feb	20
Mar	15
Apr	10
May	5
June	5
July	0
Aug	0
Sept	10
Oct	15
Nov	15
Dec	20

Data C: which place is this?

Dec 28°C   Feb 30°C
Jan 25°C   Oct 30°C   May 38°C
April 35°C   Aug 40°C
Sept 35°C   July 42°C
June 40°C   Nov 30°C
Mar 32°C

Data D: which place is this?

Did you know?

The world's hottest place is Death Valley, California, USA. Temperatures can reach over 50°C.

The world's wettest place is Tutunendo, Colombia, South America. The average monthly rainfall is over 900 mm. With no draining away or drying out, a month's rain would be over 900 mm deep.

17

A2.1 The same but different

We are all human beings. We are all the same type of animal. But we are not all exactly the same to look at. The pictures show typical fun runs. Athletes and all sorts of other people are taking part to raise money for charity.

Answer these with your group:

1 Look at the runners in the pictures. Do they have any features which are the same? List as many as you can.
2 Do the runners have any features which are different? List as many as you can.
3 See if you can add to your lists by looking at other students in your group.
4 You can control some of your features. For instance, you can change your weight by changing what you eat. Are there any other features which you can control? List them.
5 Make a list of any features which you *can't* control.
6 If you can't control some of your features, how do you think you got them?
7 You could divide the runners into two groups, male and female. How many other ways can you find to divide the runners into two groups? Make a list of your ideas.

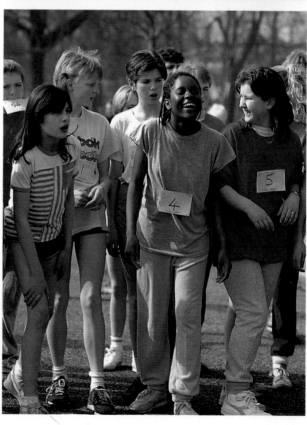

Measuring the difference

You will probably find differences between the people in your class. Differences like this are called **variations**. For example, height is one feature that shows variation.

Investigate

Investigate some of the variations between the people in your class.

Things to think about
- What feature are you going to start with?
- What measuring instruments will you need?
- How will you record the **data** (information) you need?
- How will you present your data? Would a bar chart be useful? The way you present your results will depend on the kind of data you collect. For instance, if you measure height you may collect a wide range of results. But if you are investigating colour, there are fewer choices.

What to do
- Choose one feature to study.
- Make the measurements you need and record your findings.
- Do the same for any other features you choose.
- Make a poster to present your results.
- Compare your results with those of other groups.

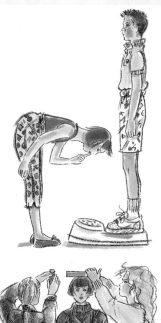

Tongue rollers

Can you roll your tongue like the person in the picture? Lots of people can't however much they practise.

Investigate

Find out how many people in your class can roll their tongue. Find out which of your relations can and which can't. Ask as many as possible as this will make the results more interesting.

What to do
- Carry out your surveys.
- Make a chart of your family showing which of your relations can roll their tongues.
- Compare your poster with others from the class. Try to find some connections between what everyone has found.
- Is it true to say that a person can roll their tongue if at least one of their parents can roll their tongue?

Do they grow the same?

Investigate

Gardeners often buy seeds by the packet. Find out whether seeds from the same packet all produce identical plants or whether there are differences between them.

You need
Seeds (for example: mustard or cress), Petri dish, cotton wool, tap water, items chosen by you.

Useful information
When seeds start to grow into seedlings (young plants), scientists say they have **germinated**.

Things to think about
- Which seeds will you choose and why?
- How many seeds will you grow and for how long?
- How can you make sure that your tests are fair? Do the growing conditions need to be the same for each seed?
- What differences will you be looking for? What measurements will you need to make and how will you record them?
- How will you present your results? Would it be useful to stick the young plants onto paper with sticky tape?

What to do
- Plan your investigations.
- Prepare the seeds in a petri dish. The pictures show you how.
- Decide when your plants are ready to be studied.
- Make a list of any differences you can see between the plants.
- Take the measurements you need and record your results.
- Did all your plants germinate?
- How did your plants vary? Make a chart to show your results.
- Write a report on what you did.
- Are there any ways in which you could improve your experiments? If so, what are they?

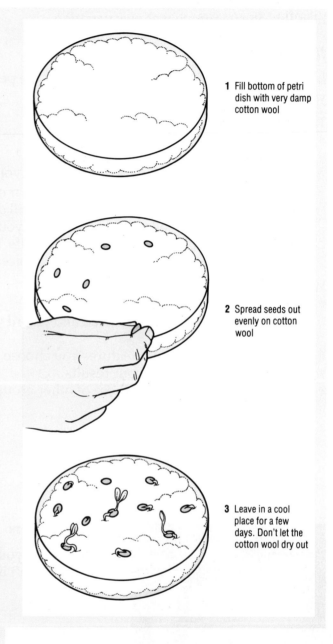

1 Fill bottom of petri dish with very damp cotton wool

2 Spread seeds out evenly on cotton wool

3 Leave in a cool place for a few days. Don't let the cotton wool dry out

Did you know?

Over a hundred years ago an Austrian monk called Gregor Mendel began measuring plant differences. He wanted to know what made plants of the same type different. He started the science called **genetics**. Today, scientists use his results to explain how plant and animal breeding works.

Animal variations

When scientists are investigating differences, they find plants easier to study than animals. For example, plants can be bred quite quickly.

- Why else do you think scientists might find plants easier to study than animals? The pictures may give you some clues.

Woodlice differences

Investigate

Collect woodlice from different places. Find out if woodlice from the same place vary and if woodlice from different places vary.

You need
Small collecting tins with air holes punched in the lid, damp leaf litter or soil, magnifying glass, ruler marked in millimetres (mm).

Useful information
There are several types of woodlice, so don't mix them up. If a woodlouse curls up when you touch it, it is a **pill woodlouse**.

Things to think about
- Where will you find the woodlice?
- How many will you collect?
- Which features are you going to investigate? Use the drawings to help you.
- How are you going to measure these features?
- How are you going to record your results?

What to do
- Collect the woodlice. Remember: all living things should be handled gently.
- Make the measurements and record your results.

What to do
- Plan your investigation.
- Find the answers to these questions:
   Are there differences between woodlice from one place?
   Are there differences between woodlice from different places?
- Present your results so that other groups can see what you have found.

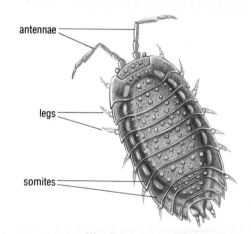

Woodlouse

Pill woodlice curl up when touched

Earthworm differences

Investigate

- Carry out an investigation on earthworms just like the one you did for woodlice. Find out if there are any differences between earthworms.

A2.3 Friends and relations

In the picture on the right, there are four mixed-up pairs of twins. With your group:

1 Decide who belongs with whom and put the names in pairs.

2 Draw a table with four columns. At the head of each column put the names of a different pair of twins. In each colummn, write in the features which made you think that those people belonged together.

Sometimes, people say that twins are identical.

3 What does 'identical twins' mean?

4 Do you think that any of the twins in the picture are identical? If so, which ones?

Where do your features come from?

You came from a tiny egg inside your mother. The egg started to grow into a baby when it was fertilized by a sperm from your father. This meant that your mother and your father each passed on some of their features to you. You **inherited** features from both parents. If you have any brothers and sisters, they also inherited features from your parents, but not exactly the same ones as you.

If you are an identical twin, you and your twin both came from the same egg. Once fertilized, this egg divided into two identical eggs which grew into two babies. So you both inherited the same features from your parents.

If you and your twin are not identical, then you came from different eggs that were fertilized by different sperm. You inherited features from your parents, but not exactly the same ones as your twin. It was just like having an ordinary brother or sister who developed at the same time as you.

5 Explain why some twins are identical twins and others are not.

Scientists know that it isn't only inherited features which decide what you are like. It also depends on where you live and the

James   Alison   Matty

Simon   Jane   Matthew

Hannah   Julian

A human ovum, seen here through a microscope, is no bigger than a full stop

condition around you. It depends on your **environment**.

6 What does the word 'environment' mean?

7 Most people can tell identical twins apart, because they don't look *exactly* the same. Why do you think there might be differences between them?

Lawrence and Paul

Lawrence and Paul are identical twins. You can see them in the pictures. Most identical twins live together in the same family. But Lawrence and Paul are different. They were separated at birth and brought up in different families.

Answer with your group:
When Lawrence and Paul have grown up,
8 which of their features might still be the same?
9 which of their features might be different?
10 do you think their personalities will be the same or different? To answer this question, think about what it might have been like if they hadn't been separated.

Paul and family

Which is which?

Below are some facts and figures about two groups of people. They were all born between 1955 and 1960. The people in one group are all cousins; they all have the same grandparents. The people in the other group are not related. See if you can work out which group is which:
11 Compare the two groups by drawing bar charts for each set of figures.
12 Decide which group of people you think might be the *cousins* and which are *unrelated*. What made you reach this decision? Explain why you are certain about your decision, or not very certain.

Lawrence and family

Group A

Name	Height in cm	Mass in kg	Eye colour	Tongue roller?
Sue	150	50	Blue	Yes
Peter	170	60	Blue	No
James	174	75	Blue	No
Carol	154	60	Brown	No
Diane	155	45	Blue	No
Brian	173	80	Brown	Yes
Jenny	152	55	Blue	No
Eric	176	65	Blue	No
Dave	172	75	Blue	No
John	171	60	Brown	No

Group B

Name	Height in cm	Mass in kg	Eye colour	Tongue roller?
Steve	160	75	Brown	Yes
Julie	152	55	Brown	Yes
Mark	180	70	Brown	Yes
Paul	184	75	Brown	Yes
Kate	164	50	Blue	No
Karen	166	60	Blue	Yes
Liz	170	55	Blue	Yes
Robin	178	75	Brown	No
Sally	156	50	Brown	Yes
Jean	150	50	Blue	No

A3.1 Featuring animals and plants

You can tell straight away what some animals are. They have features like trunks, antlers or black and white stripes which help you recognize them. If you can't recognize an animal, you can sometimes make a good guess by comparing it with other animals you already know. Some of these may have similar features. You can use this idea with plants as well.

Looking at animals

housefly	earthworm
frog	whale
human	ant
tortoise	fox
bat	slug
sparrow	crab
spider	centipede
snake	crocodile
octopus	goldfish
horse	snail

Look at the list of animals. You probably know what they all look like because you've seen them in real life or in pictures.

1. Make a card for each animal like the one below. Choose *five* features for *each* animal and write them on the card. As there are lots of animals to think about, it might help to work with other people and share your ideas.
2. Look for a feature, such as legs, which appears quite often. Put the cards for animals with this feature in one pile.
3. Look at the cards that are left. See if you can put them in piles based on other features.
4. Start again, using other features.
5. Decide which features are most useful for grouping similar animals together. Make a list of the ones you have chosen. You may find that some features, like 'having eyes', are not very useful.
6. Try putting the animal cards into groups where they have *two* features in common. Does this make it easier to put similar animals in the same group? Compare your results with other people's and share your ideas. Save these piles for later.
7. Why do you think scientists are always trying to put things into groups?

Name of animal	Features				
	1	2	3	4	5
bird	feathers	beak	tail	wings	legs

bat

spider

octopus

house-fly

centipede

goldfish

crab

More animals

Here are some more animals for you to group. You don't have to name them.

8 For each animal letter make a card of features just as you did before.

9 Add the animal cards to the piles which you worked out before.

10 Use reference books to find the names of the animals.

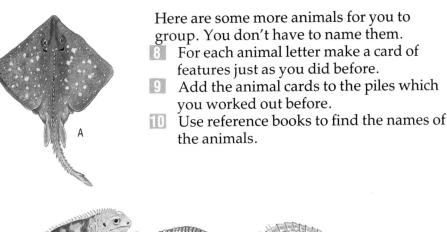

Looking at plants

Now you can try grouping the plants in the pictures. You don't have to name them.

11 The height next to each picture is the height of the *whole* plant. Put the plants into the following groups:

trees – woody plants over 4 metres tall
shrubs – woody plants under 4 metres tall
herbs – small plants that are not woody.

12 Make a list of the names of any other plants you know. Check with other people to see if they have thought of some that you have forgotten. Decide whether they are **trees**, **shrubs** or **herbs**, and put them into groups just as you did before.

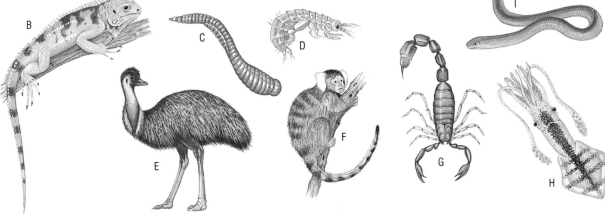

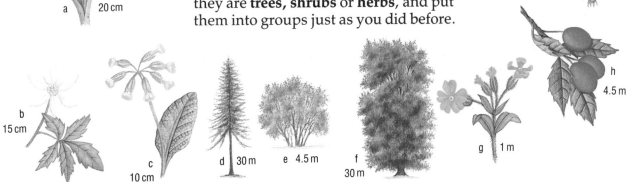

A3.2 Looking into more animals and plants

We can find out more about animals and plants by seeing what they are like inside.

1 In the past, scientists have dissected (cut open) animals to look inside them. Today they are more reluctant to dissect animals. Why do you think this is?

Looking inside animals

Look at the pictures below. They show you the insides of four different animals.

2 For each one, make a list of any parts which you recognize.

3 Make a table to show the parts which the animals have in common.

4 Which animals have the most features in common?

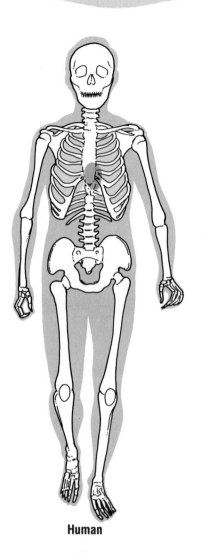

Human

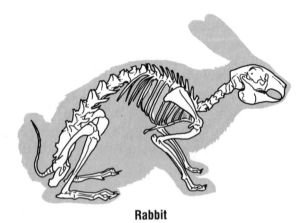

Rabbit

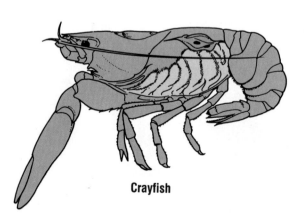

Crayfish

Chicken

Looking inside plants

Most plants are made up of roots, stems and leaves. They have to be thinly sliced to see what is inside them. This is called **sectioning**.

Investigate

Section the stems of different plants and study them through a lens or microscope.

You need
Stems, craft knife and cutting board, hand lens or microscope

What to do
- Collect some stem material from a few shrubs and herbs.
- Use craft knives to cut the stems in cross section and in vertical section. The pictures show you how to do this.
- Look at the sections using a hand lens or a microscope.
- Make large, clear drawings of everything you can see.
- Write down any features which the stems from the different plants have in common.

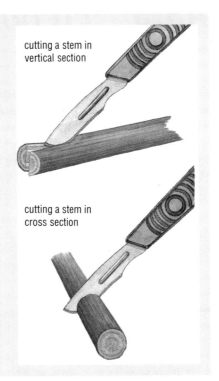

cutting a stem in vertical section

cutting a stem in cross section

Relations

Animals and plants are living things. Scientists have a name for living things. They call them **organisms**. They think that all the organisms on Earth may be related.

You may look like your cousin. This is because you share the same grandparents. You have **common ancestors**. Go back enough generations and all the people in your class may have common ancestors! Most scientists think that animals like horses and zebras have common ancestors. In fact, they think that, if you go back far enough, *all* animals have common ancestors. Generation after generation, groups of animals slowly changed and developed in their different ways. Scientists call this process **evolution**. They think that animals *and* plants may all have evolved from the same microscopic organisms that lived on Earth millions of years ago.

5 Explain what an *organism* is.
6 Explain what a *common ancestor* is.
7 What do scientists mean by *evolution*?
8 What features can you find that are similar in both animals *and* plants? The features could be how they live, how they behave or what they need, as well as how they look.

Odd one out

The plants in the pictures do not produce flowers.
9 One of the plants is an odd one out. Which one do you think it is? Explain why you chose the one you did.
10 What *habitat* would you expect each plant to have? (Look at A1.1 again if you need to find out more about habitats.)

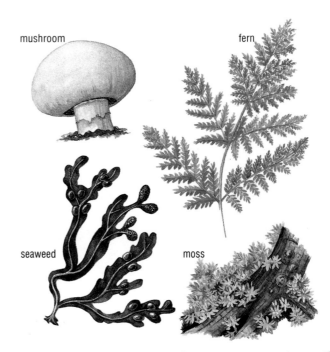

mushroom

fern

seaweed

moss

A plant which can cope with one habitat will not do as well when planted in another. Look at the pictures of the plants. The first one shows a water lily. It has large flat leaves to help it to float. This is one feature which helps the water lily live in its habitat. Helpful features like this are called **adaptations**.
With your group:

1 For each picture, write down any features which help the plant live in its habitat.

Water lily

Clematis

Cactus

Look at the pictures of the animals. The first one shows an anteater using its tongue and snout to help it seek out insects.

2 For each picture, write down any features which help the animal live in its habitat.

Anteater

Owl

Mole

Here are three more pictures of animals. The animals all have to cope with the same problem in their habitat. But they do it in different ways.

3 What is the problem?
4 What feature does each animal have to help it cope with the problem?

Walrus

Polar bear

Robin

These pictures show how some animals cope with another problem.

5 What is the problem?
6 What feature does each animal have to help it cope with the problem?

Peppered moth

Leaf insect

Chameleon

Did you know?

New life is always evolving. But many of the types of animals and plants which once lived on Earth have died out. They have become **extinct**. Today, some of the world's animals and plants are becoming very rare. Organizations like the World Wide Fund for Nature have been set up to save animals and plants threatened with extinction.

7 Can you name any animals or plants which are extinct? Make a list.
8 Can you name any animals or plants which are nearly extinct? Make a list.
9 Give some reasons why an animal or plant might become extinct.

A3.4   Making and using keys

Keys are charts, lists or diagrams which help people identify plants and animals. If you can use the features of plants and animals to sort them into groups, you can make keys for other people to use. There are several different types of key you can try out.

A branching key

Below, is a **branching key** for lawn plants. You have to look at the pictures of four lawn plants and use the key to identify them.

1 Choose one plant.
2 Start at the top of the key.
3 Work down the key, choosing the branch that describes the plant best each time.
4 Have you found the name of the plant? If so, write it down.
5 Make a list of the features which you used to identify the plant.
6 Use the key to identify the other three plants one by one.

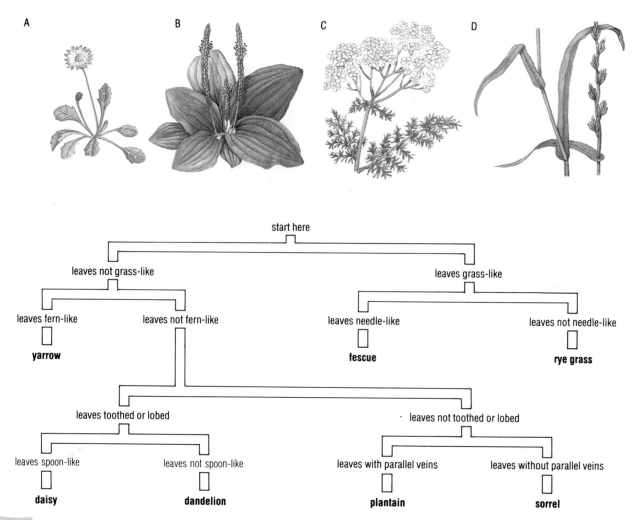

A branching key for seeds

Investigate

Make a key for four different types of seed. Test the key by getting someone else to use it. Then try making and testing a key for eight different seeds.

You need
One each of eight different types of seed.

What to do
- Start with just four seeds. Find out what types they are.
- Choose a feature that lets you divide the seeds into just *two* groups. The features list may give you some ideas.
- Draw the first two branches of your key. For example, these branches might be 'colour black' and 'colour not black'.
- Pick one of the branches. Choose two or more features that let you divide the seeds in this branch into just *two* groups. Add the new branches to your diagram. Remember to write in the names of the seeds.
- Do the same for the other branch. Your key should now be complete!
- Test your key by asking someone else to use it. Did they find the right names?
- Now make and test a branching key for *eight* seeds. You will have to add more branches this time.

Some seed features

Colour Is the seed a certain colour or not?

Size Is the seed more than a certain length (in millimetres) or not?

Grooves Does the seed have grooves or not? Does it have one groove or more than one groove?

Stripes Does the seed have stripes or not?

Shape Is the seed a particular shape or not? Examples: round, oval, kidney, pointed.

A pattern key for leaves

With a pattern key, you have to answer *yes* or *no* to a series of questions. Then you have to see which animal or plant has the matching set of answers in a table.

Investigate

Make and test a pattern key for the leaves of six trees or shrubs.

You need
Six typical leaves from six different types of tree or shrub.

What to do
- Find out the type of tree or shrub which each leaf comes from.
- Look for some features which describe each leaf. Use these features to write *four* questions. For example:
  Is the leaf shiny? Is the leaf toothed? Is the leaf round? Is the leaf hairy? Or other questions you can think of.
  The answers to each question must be a clear *yes* or *no*.
- Write out a table for your pattern key.
- Test your key by asking someone else to use it. Did they find the right names?

How to use a pattern key
Imagine you have a tortoise, a rabbit and a guinea pig, but you don't know which is which. A pattern key will tell you the answer.

Choose one of the animals. Answer *yes* or *no* to each of these questions:
1 Does it have a shell?
2 Does it have fur?
3 Does it have long ears?

Pattern key: answer table

question			animal
1	2	3	
yes	no	no	tortoise
no	yes	yes	rabbit
no	yes	no	guinea pig

A3.5   The family of life

Scientists believe that all of the animals and plants on Earth are related. To show how closely they are related, they try to put them into groups.

Look at the living things in the pictures. (The organisms in the circles can only be seen through a microscope.)

1 Put the living things into *three* groups. Use the idea that things which have similar features are related. Make a table to show your three groups. Remember to put a heading at the top of each column to describe that group.

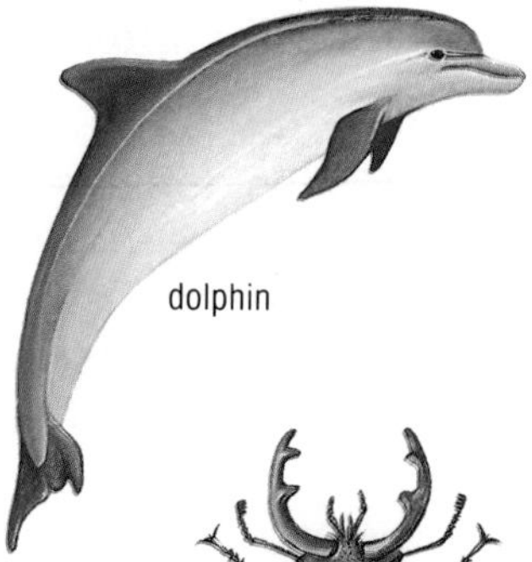

dolphin

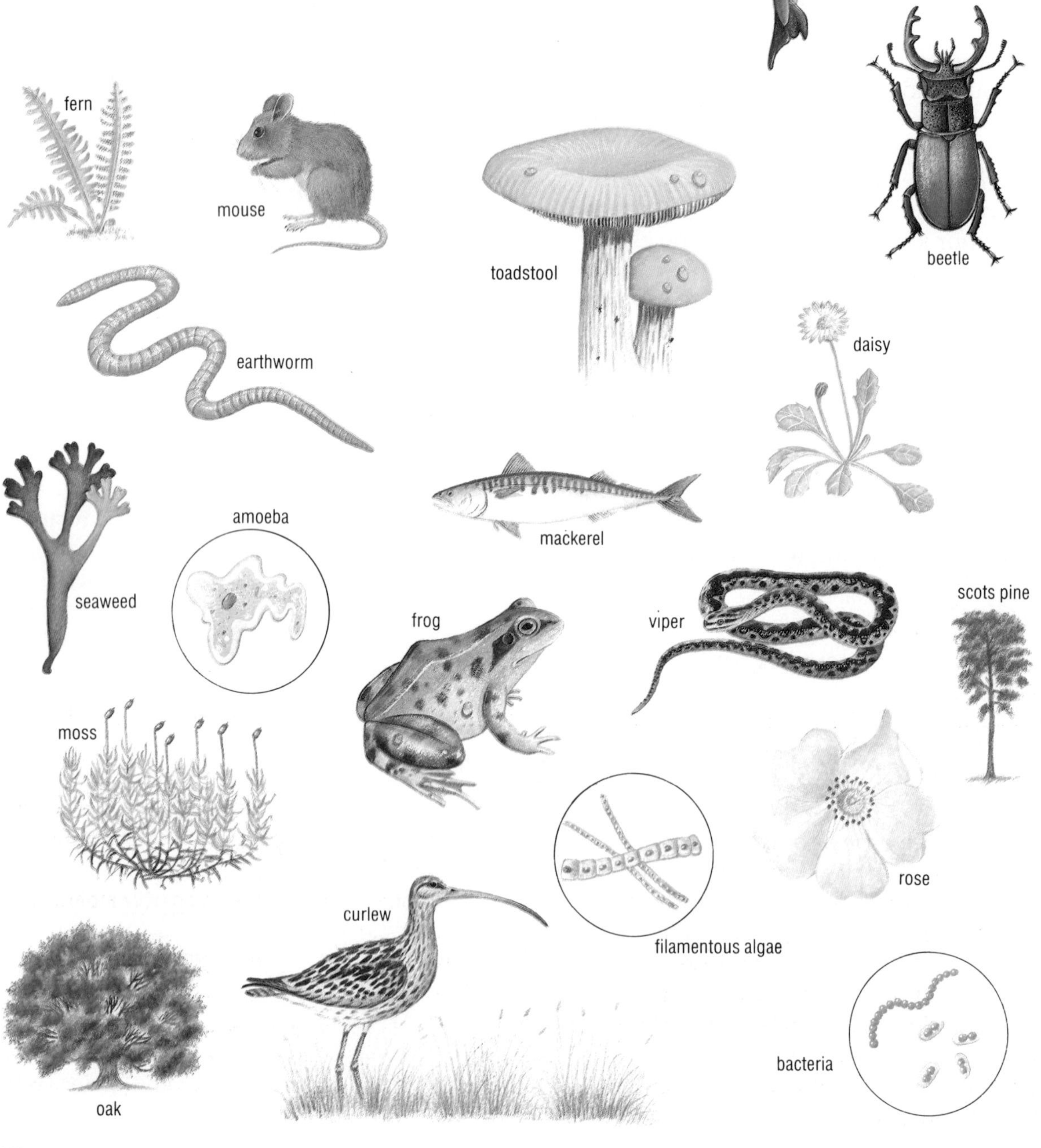

beetle

fern

mouse

toadstool

daisy

earthworm

seaweed

amoeba

mackerel

scots pine

frog

viper

moss

rose

curlew

filamentous algae

oak

bacteria

Animals with backbones

Many animals have backbones. Scientists call these animals **vertebrates** because the word vertebrate means 'having a spine'. Most scientists divide the vertebrates into five main groups: **fish, amphibians, reptiles, birds** and **mammals**.

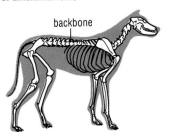

backbone

Below, is a table showing the five main groups of vertebrates.

2 Copy the table carefully. Complete your table by putting a tick (√) or a cross (×) into each space. A tick means that animals in that group mostly have that feature. A cross means they don't. Use the pictures and the information to help you decide.

3 Check your results with others people's. Do you all agree?

4 Humans are vertebrates. What group do you think we are in?

5 Try to find some other examples of animals in each group. Make lists of them.

Feature	Fish	Amphibians	Reptiles	Birds	Mammals
backbone					
fins					
scales					
lay eggs					
have babies					
hair					
damp skin					
feathers					
mammary glands					
gills					
lungs					
steady body temperature					

Information
- Vertebrates which spend all their time living and breathing underwater have gills for breathing. The other vertebrates have lungs.
- Most of the vertebrates lay eggs. But mammals are different. Most of them give birth to live young. They produce 'babies'.
- One group of animals has hairy skin. Sometimes, there is very little hair. But if there is lots, we call it fur.
- Like others in their group, frogs and toads have skin which feels damp to touch.
- Cows, like other mammals, have mammary glands which produce milk for their young.
- We keep a steady temperature inside our bodies. But some of the vertebrates are not like this. Fish, amphibians and reptiles have a body temperature that changes. It depends on their surroundings and how active they are.

Stepping stones

Dave's house

Dave lives in an old house in the country. The doors and windows don't fit very well, so insects and other small animals are always getting in.

1 Make a list of all the animals that Dave might find in his house and garden. Write down the habitats they might be in. Your list could start like this:

animal	habitat
spider	loft

Keeping out the flies

Dave gets lots of flies in his house. He wants to attract them out of his kitchen and into the garden. One friend says that flies are attracted to jam. Another friend says that they prefer cheese.

2 How could Dave find out? Design an experiment for him; describe what he has to do and draw the equipment. Remember: flies are very difficult to catch. And Dave doesn't want to sit around all day waiting to see them.

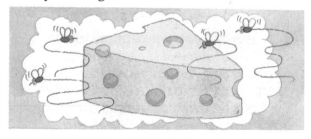

Summer and winter

Dave sees lots of butterflies in his garden in the summer. He can't understand why they all vanish in the winter and then appear again the following spring.

3 How would you explain to Dave what is going on.

Dave's garden is different in the winter to in the summer.

4 How many differences can you think of? Make a list.

Neighbour problems

Dave's neighbour is friendly, but not very considerate. There are lots of ways in which he pollutes Dave's habitat.

5 List all the things that Dave might want his neighbour to stop doing.

Up the wall

Dave bought a packet of flower seeds and scattered them all round the garden. He can't understand why they have grown to different sizes if they all came from the same packet.

6 Write a letter to Dave, explaining why.

Tess and Tiger

Dave has two pets: a dog called Tess and a cat called Tiger.

7 What things about Tess and Tiger are the *same*? List as many as you can.

8 What things about Tess and Tiger are *different*? List as many as you can.

Tiger isn't the only cat around. There are at least ten others in Dave's area. They all look much the same because they are all cats. But they don't look *exactly* the same.

9 Make a list of all the things that might be different about the cats.

Tess and Tiger both belong to the same group of vertebrates.

10 Why are they called vertebrates?

11 What group of vertebrates do they belong to?

12 What group of vertebrates does Dave belong to?

Which is which?

Dave has seen a reptile and an amphibian in his garden.

13 What two animals might he have seen? Which is the reptile and which is the amphibian?

What's the insect?

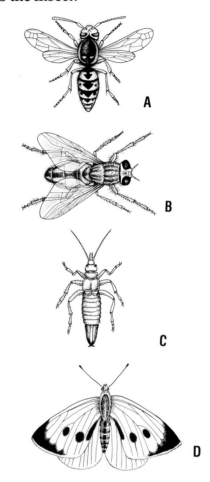

Dave has found a lot of insects in his garden. He has looked up their names in a book. He has made a key so that visitors can work out what they are as well.

14 Here is Dave's key. Use it to find the name of each insect:

1	Wings	Go to 2
	No wings to be seen	Earwig
2	Two pairs of wings	Go to 3
	One pair of wings	Housefly
3	Wings larger than body	Butterfly
	Wings not larger than body	Wasp

B Microbes and health

The pictures below are in pairs. Between each 'before' and 'after' picture, there has been a change. With your group, answer these questions about the pictures:

Sarah's mother mixed some things together in a big bucket. Three weeks later her brown liquid had a very different taste.

1 What was Sarah's mother making?

2 Can you name any of the things which she put in the bucket? What were they?

3 Look at the two pictures. How many differences can you see? Make a list.

Before . . .   **. . . after**

Sarah mixed up some dough. Some time later, the dough had changed into a loaf of bread.

4 What ingredients might Sarah have used in the dough?

5 What did Sarah do to the dough to turn it into bread?

6 Look at the two pictures. How many differences can you see? Make a list.

Before . . .   **. . . after**

It started off as a large jug of milk. Some time later the milk had turned into a block of cheese.

7 This cheese has a special feature. What is it?

8 Look at the two pictures. How many differences can you see? Make a list.

Now look at all the 'after' pictures down the right-hand side of the page.

9 Can you find any features which are the same in all of them? If so, what are they?

Before . . .   **. . . after**

Microbes in action

Scientists think that beer, bread and cheese are all made when tiny things called **microbes** get to work. Microbes are living things, but they are really too small to be called either animals or plants. The ones in the picture were photographed through a microscope. There are many types of microbes. They can be found in plants, animals, food, water, and even floating around in the air. You can even buy them in packets!

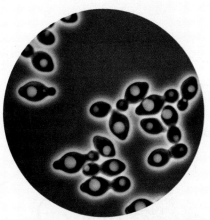

Microbes magnified 900 times

Investigate

Find out whether microbe paste shows signs of life. Find out what happens to the microbe paste when it is given some food.

You need
Microbe paste, sugar, water, flour, two test tubes, pipette, spatula, stirring rod, two microscope slides, microscope, beaker.

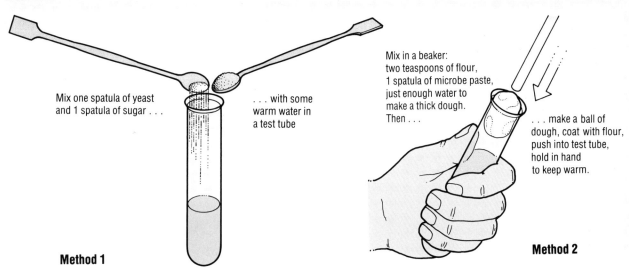

Mix one spatula of yeast and 1 spatula of sugar . . .

. . . with some warm water in a test tube

Method 1

Mix in a beaker:
two teaspoons of flour,
1 spatula of microbe paste,
just enough water to
make a thick dough.
Then . . .

. . . make a ball of dough, coat with flour, push into test tube, hold in hand to keep warm.

Method 2

What to do
- A cat and a tree are both living things. Think of all the features which make something alive. Make a list of them.
- Look at your microbe paste. Is it doing any of the things on your list?
- Try feeding your microbe paste in two ways:
  1 with sugar and water   **2** with flour and water.
  The diagrams show you how.
- In each experiment, check the mixture every ten minutes. Is anything happening? Make a note of everything you see.
- Is the microbe paste showing signs of being alive? If so, what signs?
- Take some runny mixture from the test tube in Method 1. You can use a pipette for this. Put the drop between two microscope slides and look at it through a microscope. Draw what you see. Did you find any blobs like the microbes in the photograph?

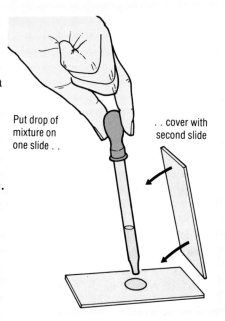

Put drop of mixture on one slide . .

. . cover with second slide

B1.2 A problem with drink

Ig's or Og's?

Og, the caveman, has collected a huge supply of apples. There are far too many for him to eat. But he has an idea. He will crush up the apples to make juice so that he can put it in a container he has invented. He's called it a bottle!

The bottle of apple juice has been standing in the sun for a few days. Og is very surprised when the top flies off and the juice bubbles out. 'What can have caused that?' he thinks.

Ig also has a pile of apples, but he doesn't like apple skins so he is peeling all his apples first. Ig crushes the apples like Og did and then fills his bottles with the juice. Nothing happens to Ig's bottles.

1 What has Ig done differently to Og?
2 What made Og's juice bubble up?
3 What does this tell you about apple skins?

Investigate

From two samples of juice, find out which is Og's and which is Ig's.

You need
2 samples of apple juice, 2 test tubes and corks.

Things to think about
* How will you compare the two juices? You must not taste either of them because they might be poisonous.
* How will you decide which juice is which?

What to do
Warning! Don't put corks in test tubes too tightly.
■ Compare the two juices. Make a list of the differences between them.
■ Decide which is Og's juice and which is Ig's.
■ Explain how you reached your conclusion.

Yeast at work

Many microbes float around in the air and stick to plants and fruits. Yeast is a microbe like this. It was yeast which made Og's juice bubble up. The yeast in the picture was photographed through a microscope. Each tiny round bit is called a yeast cell.

4 Do you recognize the picture? What do you think was in the microbe paste which you used in the investigation you did before?

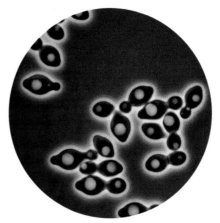

Yeast cells magnified 900 times

Yeast and sugar

Og has experimented with juices from grapes, pears, blackcurrants, strawberries, carrots and potatoes. They've all blown the tops off the bottles. Og thinks that the juices bubble because yeast feeds on the sugar in the fruit and vegetables. Ig thinks yeast would grow just as well with only water.

Investigate

Is Og right? Does yeast feed on sugar, or does it just need water?

You need
Sugar, water, beaker, spatula, stirring rod, yeast, 2 test tubes.

Things to think about
• How can you tell if the yeast is alive?

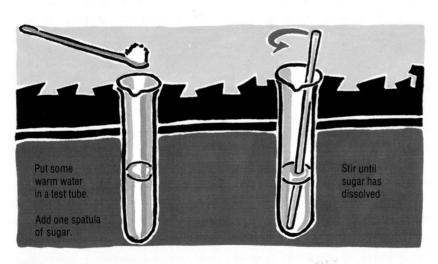

Put some warm water in a test tube.

Add one spatula of sugar.

Stir until sugar has dissolved

What to do
- Plan your investigation.
- Mix up some sugar and warm water to make a sugar solution. The diagram shows you how.
- Carry out your investigations.
- You were told to use warm water. But would it matter if the water was cold, or hot? Carry out some more investigations to find out.
- Make a poster to show all your findings.

Did you know?

When Og's fruit juices are bubbling away, scientists say that they are **fermenting**. During **fermentation**, the yeast feeds on the sugar in the fruit and changes it into **alcohol**. A gas called **carbon dioxide** is given off at the same time. Nowadays, people buy Og's fermented juices in bottles. They call it wine.

B1.3 Making the bread

Missing ingredient

Barry decides to make his own bread. When the loaf comes out of the oven, it is crusty and brown. Barry is happy because the dough has risen and the bread is light and full of air. He tries making another loaf but, oh dear, this turns out flat and hard. 'I must have left out one of the ingredients,' says Barry.

Investigate

Find out which ingredient Barry might have forgotten when he made his bread.

You need
Ingredients given in Barry's recipe, large beaker or bowl, spatula or spoon, baking tray or sheet of kitchen foil.

Things to think about
- Is there more than one ingredient which Barry might have forgotten?
- How many samples of bread will you need to make? Will you leave any ingredients out each time? If so, how many?
- How will you make sure that your tests are fair?
- Will you bake your bread?

What to do
- Plan your investigation.
- Mix your doughs and bake your bread. The diagrams show you how. **Warning!** You must not eat any bread made in the laboratory.
- Carry out your investigation and record all your findings.
- Write a letter to Barry telling him which ingredient he might have left out of his bread. Explain your reasons to him.

BREAD
100g plain flour
2g salt
2g butter
5g dried yeast
2g sugar
60 ml water

1 Weigh out ingredients. Using a warm bowl, mix flour, salt, butter. Then add water (at 35°C), sugar, yeast.

2 When dough is soft, knead on dry surface

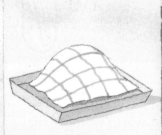

3 Cover with damp cloth. Leave for 1 hour in a warm place.

4 Knead again. Then put in oven for 15 minutes at 230 °C.

Raising the dough

Sian has noticed that dough gets larger when it is left to stand. She wonders where the best place is to keep her dough when she leaves it to stand. Barry suggests that the dough should be kept cool. Sara thinks that the dough needs to be in a warm place. Who is right?

Investigate

Find out if dough rises best if it is kept in a warm place.

You need
Fresh dough (look back at Barry's recipe), kitchen foil or some pieces of clean cloth, bunsen burner, bench mat.

Things to think about
- Where will you put the dough to keep it cool?
- Where will you put your dough to keep it warm?
- How are you going to compare your doughs?

What to do
- Plan your investigation.
- Mix your dough and carry out your investigation.
- What did you find?
- How did your results compare with other groups'?

At the baker's

Bread can be baked in many different ways.

1. How many different types of bread can you see in the picture? Make a list.
2. Not all breads are full of tiny holes. What 'unrisen' breads can you see in the picture? Why are they like this?
3. Collect some bread wrappers and look at the list of ingredients on each. What substances are listed that are not in Barry's recipe? What do you think these extra ingredients are for?

Did you know?

The flour in dough has a soft, rubbery substance in it called **gluten**. When bread is baked the gluten becomes hard and rigid. It traps the gas produced by the yeast. This is why most breads have holes in them.

Say cheese

Ciaran is visiting a cheesemaker to find out how milk is turned into cheese. The cheesemaker tells him that microbes in the milk turn it sour. Sour milk has lumpy bits in it which microbes turn into cheese. A liquid called **rennet** is added to the milk to help the microbes do their job, Ciaran wants to know what effect the rennet has.

Investigate

Find out what effect rennet has on milk.

You need
Milk, rennet, test tubes, pipette, beaker, warm water.

Useful information
- Milk is a mixture of many different substances. **Curds** are the solid, fatty substances that microbes turn into cheese. **Whey** is a watery liquid that isn't much use except as food for pigs! In ordinary milk, these are all mixed up so that the milk is a smooth liquid.

Things to think about
- Will you try mixing different amounts of rennet with milk?
- Will you try the effects of adding rennet to cold milk and to warm milk? The diagram shows you a way of warming milk gently. What will happen to the microbes in milk if you heat them too much?
- How often will you check to see what is happening to the milk?
- If you are comparing the effects of rennet, how can you be sure your tests are fair?

What to do
- Plan your investigation.
- Ask your teacher to check your plan.
- Carry out your investigation.
- Watch carefully to see what happens to the milk in each of your tests. Keep a record of what you see.
- Write a letter to Ciaran telling him what you did and what you found out. Include some drawings if it would make things clearer.

Making cheese

milk ——— ———warm water

Enzymes in action

Rennet contains a substance called **rennin** which helps milk separate into curds and whey more quickly. Scientists have a word for substances like rennin which speed up changes. They call them **enzymes**. Enzymes are natural substances from animals and plants.

Did you know?

Some microbes occur naturally in milk. Others are mixed in by the cheesemaker. More may be added later so that the cheese develops special features like blue 'veins' or holes (formed by gas bubbles).

Made by microbes?

Microbes are involved in making many different foods. For example, cheese and yoghurt are both made when microbes get to work on milk. Look at the pictures below. They show different types of food (the drinks are really a type of food as well).

1. Which of the foods were made starting with milk?
2. Which of the foods were made with the help of microbes?

Some of the foods were made using yeast.

3. In which foods was yeast used?
4. What did the yeast do to each of these foods?

Missing microbes

Imagine that you are an astronaut setting up a base on another planet. There are no microbes on the planet but you have a good supply of basic foods like fruit, flour and milk.

5. Write a message asking for a supply of microbes. You must tell ground control what you are going to do with the microbes and why you need them.

Put it away!

With your group, look at the big picture. It shows part of Mr and Mrs Robinson's kitchen.

1 Make a list of all the places in the kitchen where food might be stored.

Mr and Mrs Robinson have just gone on their summer holiday. They will be away for three weeks. They didn't eat up all their food before they left. And they forgot to put some of it away.

2 Look at the picture and see if you can find the following:
> an apple
> an open, half-empty bottle of milk
> a crust of bread
> a tin of peas
> a piece of cheese
> a bowl of dog food
> an open packet of biscuits
> a banana
> carrots
> potatoes
> a packet of crisps

3 What do you think will happen to each of the above foods during the time the Robinsons are away?

4 Imagine that the Robinsons have gone away in winter instead of summer. Will the same thing happen to their food? What difference will it make?

Shopping trip

The Robinsons have returned from their holiday. They stop at a supermarket to buy some more food. You can see their shopping list on the right.

5 Where should they store each item of food when they get home so that it can be kept fresh?

In and out of the garden

Mr Robinson is peeling the potatoes for lunch. Mrs Robinson is out in the garden cutting the grass, which has grown very long while they have been away. The Robinsons have a compost heap at the bottom of their garden. Mrs Robinson puts the grass cuttings on the compost heap. Then Mr Robinson puts the potato peelings on as well.

6 What happens to the grass cuttings and the potato peelings when they are left on the compost heap?

7 Why do the Robinsons keep a compost heap?

When lunch is ready, Mrs Robinson comes in from the garden. The first thing she does is to wash her hands.

8 Why does she wash her hands?

9 What could happen if she didn't wash her hands before eating?

Shopping list.

loaf of bread
pint of milk
fresh sausages
packet of frozen peas
cheese
tins dog food
tin baked beans
½ dozen eggs
cabbage
6 apples
packet frozen chips
crisps

B2.2   Problems with milk

Off milk

Mr Green sells milk in his shop. Recently he has been having complaints from his customers. He decides to write to the Public Health Inspector:

Dear Inspector,

Some of my customers have complained that the milk I have sold them is 'off.' My milk comes from three different dairies: Milkco Dairies, Cow and Cream Dairies, and Farm Fresh Dairy. I don't know which one is sending the 'off' milk. Can you help me find which dairy it is?

Yours sincerely,
D. Green.
(Green's Grocers)

Investigate

Imagine that you are the Health Inspector. Help Mr Green to find out which dairy is supplying the milk which has gone off.

You need
Samples of fresh and old milk, and milk from the three dairies, bacteria indicator, beaker, pipette, test tubes.

Useful information

- **Bacteria** are a type of microbe. Even fresh milk has some bacteria in it. As more and more bacteria grow in milk, it goes 'off'.

- If you add a few drops of bacteria indicator to milk, its colour may change. It depends on how many bacteria there are in the milk.

Things to think about
- How will you be able to tell if milk from one of the dairies is 'off'? Will you need to do any other tests first?
- Bacteria indicator needs to be at about the temperature of hand-warm water to work properly. How will you keep the milk warm?

What to do
- Plan your investigation.
- Ask your teacher to check your plan.
- Carry out your investigation. To use the indicator, put a few drops into a test tube half full of milk and see what happens.
- Which of the milk samples was 'off'? Write a letter to Mr Green telling him what you found.

Bacteria get hungry too!

Scientists have found that there are many types of bacteria in milk which has gone off. These bacteria produce enzymes that alter the milk so that the bacteria can use it as food. The changes in the milk make it smell. The enzymes also produce substances that can make you ill, so you should not drink milk that has gone off.

Keeping milk fresh

When Mr Green goes camping, he sometimes collects his milk in a jug from a local farm. He likes the taste of the milk, but finds that it goes off very quickly. Perhaps this is because the jug is not sealed like a milk bottle or carton. Or perhaps it is because the farm isn't heat-treating the milk. Mr Green knows that milk from dairies is heated before it goes into cartons and bottles.

Investigate

Investigate some different ways of making milk stay fresh longer.

You need
Milk, test tubes, items chosen by you.

Things to think about
- How can you test Mr Green's ideas?
- Can you try any other way of keeping the milk fresh?
- How can you make sure that your tests are fair?
- Boiling alters the taste of the milk. If you are going to heat milk, how can you do this without boiling it?
- What will you need to test your milk samples?
- How long will you leave your milk samples before testing them. How often will you test them?
- How will you record your results?

What to do
- Plan your investigation.
- Make a list of the items you need.
- Ask your teacher to check your plan.
- Carry out your investigation. What ways did you find of making milk stay fresh longer?
- Display your findings by making a poster called 'Keeping milk fresh'.

Did you know?

Pasteurised milk has been treated by heating it to 70°C for about 15 seconds. This kills off most of the bacteria.
Sterilised 'long life' milk has been heated to over 100°C for longer. This kills off all the bacteria, but alters the taste.

Bacteria magnified 3800 times

Do you know which of these milks are pasteurized?
Do you know what the colours of the tops mean?

B2.3 Stopping the rot

If you look carefully at the labels of food packets you will find that they are marked with 'sell by', 'use by', or 'best before' dates. These are the dates by which the food should be sold, used or eaten. After these dates the food may not be nice or even safe to eat. Answer these with your group:

1 What makes the food turn nasty?

2 Why do you think some foods have 'sell by' or 'use by' dates, while other foods have 'best before' dates? Make a survey of foods at home which have the different types of date.

3 Many tinned foods and packets of dried food do not have these dates on them. Why not?

Look for the dates

Sort the dates

The computer at Burtons supermarket went wrong. It failed to print the dates on some food labels. Debbie Jones, the manager, had a list of the dates but did not know which foods they belonged to.

4 See if you can solve the problem.

Rotten apples

Mr and Mrs Robinson have picked some apples from their tree and left them in their kitchen. A few days later they notice that some of the apples have brown spots on them.

Investigate

Look at the brown spots under a microscope to see what is making the apple rot.

You need
Bad apples, spatula or knife, microscope slides, microscope.

Useful information
Apples rot because microbes get to work on them. Some of these microbes are bacteria. Others are called **fungi** ('funguses'). These are the microbes you might be able to see through the microscope. Yeast is a type of fungus.

What to do
- Use a microscope to compare some fresh apple and some rotting apple.
- Describe and draw what you see.
- Write a letter to the Robinsons explaining what is happening to their apples.

2 June
5 June
12 June
14 June
1 July
4 July
31 Aug
Oct 1990
Nov 1990
June 1991

Debbie's list of dates, written on the 1st June, 1990.

Carton of milk
Fresh eggs
Corn flakes
Carton of orange juice
Fruit yoghurt
Cheddar cheese
Shortcake biscuits
Sliced loaf
Can of lemonade
Prepacked bacon

Items of food without dates

Did you know?

Not all microbes make food bad. Some of them make cheese and yoghurt!

Apples in store

The Robinsons want to keep their apples as long as possible without them turning bad. Perhaps you can solve their problem. Here's a way of starting:

5 Make a list of the methods used to stop food rotting. Sometimes the food may be kept as it is. Sometimes it may be **processed** (changed) by doing things to it or mixing things with it. The picture might give you some clues.

6 Make a list of the methods that might be used to keep apples fit to eat.

Some ways of helping to stop food rotting

Investigate

Try some methods of storing apples and find out how well they work.

You need
Fresh apples, knife, jars, kitchen foil or cling film, beakers, bunsen burner, tripod, gauze, bench mat, use of a 'fridge, items chosen by you.

Things to think about
● What methods will you try?
● If you are comparing different methods, how will you make sure that your tests are fair?
● How long will you leave the apples?
● How much apple will you use for each method?
● Will you need any other substances?
● How can you tell whether the apples are fit to eat? (You must not taste them.)

What to do
▥ Plan your tests.
▥ Make a list of the items you need.
▥ Ask your teacher to check your plan.
▥ Carry out your tests. Keep a record of all your findings.
▥ Make a poster about storing apples. Use it to say which methods you found best.

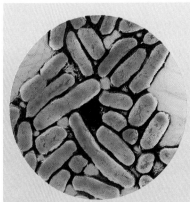
Salmonella bacteria magnified 6800 times

Did you know?

Salmonella is a harmful microbe which can thrive in meat and eggs which have not been stored, prepared or cooked properly. In Britain, it causes over 6000 cases of food poisoning every year.

Juicy fruit

The Robinsons also buy fresh apple juice in cartons from the supermarket.

7 See if you can find out what manufacturers do to apple juice to make sure it stays fresh in the carton.

8 What will happen to the apple juice if it is left open and out of the 'fridge for a long time?

9 Draw a poster warning people of the danger of eating food that harmful microbes have been growing on. Suggest ways of keeping these microbes away from food.

B2.4   Rotting away

The picture shows Mr and Mrs Robinson's garden. It is next to a farm.

1 Make a table of all the things in the picture which are rotting. Give the reason why you chose each one. You could start your table like this:

Rotting thing	Reason for choosing
Apple on ground	Gone brown

2 What happens to all the 'stuff' in something when it rots? Where do you think it all goes?

Gardeners say that plants can't grow without 'goodness' from the soil. This 'goodness' is substances in the soil called **nutrients**. As the Robinsons' apple tree grows, it takes nutrients out of the soil. Answer these with your group:

3 The Robinsons pick and eat most of their apples. What happens to the nutrients in them?

4 What happens to the nutrients in the apples which drop to the ground and rot?

5 The farmer next door grows lots of fruit and vegetables to be sold. She sometimes puts bags of fertilizers on the soil. And she sometimes spreads muck from her cows and pigs. Why do you think she does this?

The compost heap

The Robinsons have a compost heap in of their garden. On it they put grass cuttings, potato peelings, old apples and anything else which will rot. Every couple of years, when the compost heap has rotted right down, Mrs Robinson digs the compost into the soil.

6 Why do you think she does this?

Some things are good for a compost heap and some things are harmful.

7 Make a table to show which waste things you would put on a compost heap and which things you would not. The photo at the bottom of the page may give you some ideas.

Likes and dislikes

Materials rot when microbes get to work on them. Microbes are living things. Some conditions help them to survive and some things don't. If the conditions are right, the number of microbes grows and grows. The microbes **multiply**.

Think about the work you have done so far in this module. Then see if you can answer these questions about the conditions microbes prefer. (There are some clues after the questions.)

8 Do microbes like to be warm or cold?
9 Do microbes like moisture or do they prefer to be dry?
10 Do microbes need air (because of the oxygen in it), or do they prefer to have no air?

Here are some clues to help you answer the questions.
- Milk doesn't keep very well if it is left on the doorstep in the summer.
- Half-empty bottles of wine don't keep very well.
- Fresh tea-bags can be stored for a long time. Used tea bags from a teapot will rot if put on a compost heap.

Muck spreading on the farm

Did you know?

Scientists have a word to describe materials which rot away. They say that they are **biodegradable**. Things which won't rot away are **non-biodegradable**.

11 Which of the things in the picture are biodegradable?
12 Non-biodegradable things can be a nuisance. Why do you think this is?
13 Make a poster to show the difference between biodegradable and non-biodegradable materials.

Will they rot or not?

Compost heaps are full of bacteria which feed on dead plants. The dead plants slowly go black and mushy. Some of the plants rot so much that they become liquid.

When people dig compost back into their soil it forms a soft, dark material called **humus**. Humus is the part of the soil which has all the nutrients.

1 Soil has humus in it, even if people don't dig in compost. Why do you think this is?

There are some blank spaces in the diagram on the right. If the diagram was finished, it would show how nutrients pass from plants back into the soil to be used again.

2 Copy the diagram. Complete your diagram by putting the words beneath it in the correct spaces.

3 Some people say that compost heaps are a way of 'recycling Nature's goodness'. What do you think they mean?

A soil problem

The Robinsons don't seem to be able to grow very good vegetables at the bottom of their garden. Mrs Robinson thinks that there might be less humus in the soil there. Is she right?

Investigate

Compare two samples of soil from the garden. Find out if there is less humus in one sample than the other.

You need
Two samples of dry soil, tin lid, items chosen by you.

Useful information
- Humus burns. The other materials in soil don't. So you can get rid of the humus in a soil sample by burning it.

Things to think about
- Would it be useful to find the mass of humus (in grams) in each sample?
- What measurements will you need to make?
- How will you record your results?

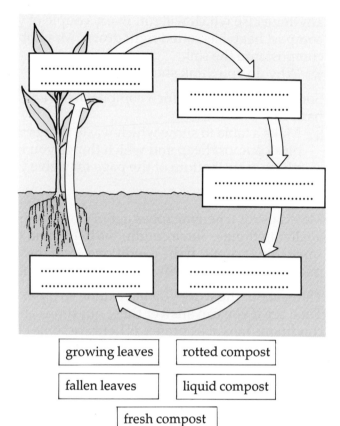

| growing leaves | rotted compost |

| fallen leaves | liquid compost |

| fresh compost |

Good soil has plenty of humus in it

What to do
- Plan your investigation.
- Make a list of any equipment you need.
- Carry out your investigation and record your results.
- Was there a difference in the amount of humus in the two samples?
- The soil in your investigation needed to be completely dry. Why was this?

Will it rot?

Here are some descriptions of a compost heap:

- **A** Pressed down to squeeze out all the air.
- **B** Kept very cold during a long winter.
- **C** Spiked with a garden fork to let air in.
- **D** Sprayed with disinfectant to get rid of the smell.
- **E** Warmed up during a hot summer.

Look at these descriptions. Think about the conditions which will help bacteria survive and multiply. Then answer these questions:

- Which descriptions help a compost heap to rot more quickly?
- Which descriptions might stop a compost heap rotting?

Food chains

Lots of things live and feed near the Robinsons' compost heap. The diagram on the right shows how nutrients pass from one living thing to another. It is called a food chain. The first arrow shows you that leaves are the food for snails.

4 What does the second arrow show you?

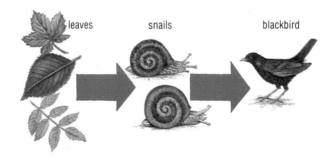

leaves   snails   blackbird

Here are some more of the feeding relationships in the Robinsons' garden:

Foxes eat moles
Worms eat leaves
Moles eat worms
Bacteria feed on dead foxes

5 Use this information to make a food chain. Remember: the arrows always go from the food to the feeder.

Habitats are places where animals and plants live, feed and grow. Walls, trees, hedges, meadows and ponds are all habitats for living things.

6 Choose *three* habitats. Make a list of the plants and animals you might find in each.
7 For each habitat, make a food chain from the plants and animals you have listed.

No ARTIFICIAL COLOURING
No ARTIFICIAL FLAVOURING

Heroin screws you up

Half the fat of butter and margarine

Look after your heart

THE SWEET TASTE OF SUMMER

Smoking can cause fatal diseases

REAL DAIRY CREAM

Drinking and driving wrecks lives

FILLS THE HUNGER GAP

One pint of beer, two glasses of wine, it's all the same to your liver

MADE FROM PURE SUNFLOWER OIL

HIGH IN POLYUNSATURATES

Look at the advertisements on the opposite page and answer these with your group.

1 Some of the advertisements are selling things.
What are they selling?
How is each one trying to encourage you to buy that thing?

2 Some of the advertisements are warning of dangers. Make a list of the dangers you are being warned about.

3 Design your own advertisement telling people how they can keep as fit and healthy as possible.

Look at the picture above. It shows all sorts of people talking to each other. There are 'speech bubbles' to show you what they are saying.

4 Decide whether you agree or disagree with each statement.

5 Choose *five* of the statements and explain why you agree or disagree with each one.

6 Find any pairs of statements which seem to say opposite things.

7 Someone says 'Surely they can't *both* be right?' Why can people sometimes say opposite things?

Lots of lovely foods. But some are better for you than others. The things you eat and drink are called your **diet**.

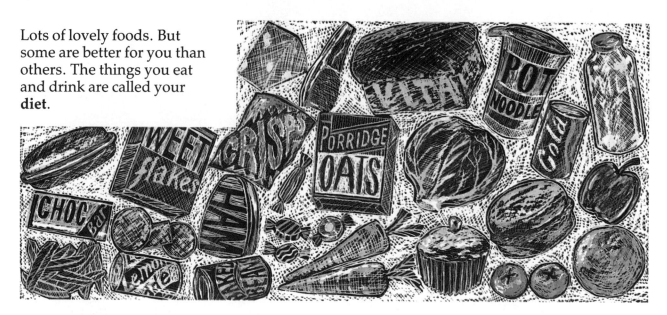

A healthy diet

Donna went to a talk in school about food. This is what she wrote after the talk:

Doctors think that most people have too much fat in their diet. They eat too many beefburgers, sausages, chips and other fried foods. This makes them more likely to develop heart disease when they get older. Most people don't eat enough fresh fruit and vegetables. Fruit and vegetables have plenty of vitamins and fibre in them. So does wholemeal bread. Fibre clears out your system and stops you getting constipated. It may also stop you getting diseases in your bowels. People take in lots more sugar than they should. Sweets, chocolates and canned drinks are full of sugar. So are most cakes and biscuits. Sugar can make you fat. It also helps bacteria rot your teeth.

You have to plan out *all* your meals, drinks *and* snacks for three days.

1. Make a plan for the three days so that your diet is as healthy as possible. The picture and Donna's notes might help you decide what to have and what to avoid.
2. A friend of yours isn't sure what foods he should cut down on. Make a plan to show your friend what a three-day diet would be like if it was as *un*healthy as possible.

Microbes at home

There are microbes floating around in the air. Some of these microbes are bacteria. They get on your hands and they can get onto your food. Some are in food already and will make it rot. Bacteria will multiply fast if the conditions are right. If they get into your body some of them can make you ill.

3. Do bacteria need to be warm to multiply or cold?
4. Why should food not be left uncovered?
5. Why should some foods be kept in a 'fridge?

Chemicals such as disinfectants kill bacteria and other microbes. People sometimes call them 'germ killers'. They use them to clean their kitchens, bathrooms and toilets.

6. Make a survey of all the things you can buy which will kill bacteria in the home.

A mouldy problem

The school caretaker has found some mould growing on a wall. He has some disinfectant that will kill the mould but the label has come off and he doesn't know how much to use. He wants to use as little as possible because the disinfectant is expensive.

Investigate

Help the caretaker. Find out the smallest amount of disinfectant needed to kill some of the mould.

You need
Mould solution (mould in some water), Janus green liquid, pipette or measuring cylinder, test tubes, disinfectant.

Useful information
- The mould on the wall is full of microbes. The microbes in this case are fungi.
- Janus green is an **indicator**. It will tell you if the microbes are alive or dead. It turns purple-red (in 5 minutes or so) if the microbes are alive. It stays blue-green if they are dead. The diagram shows you how to use Janus green.

Things to think about
- How much disinfectant will you add to the mould solution? You could start with 1 ml or 20 drops.
- Will you go on adding more and more disinfectant to one sample of mould solution? Or will you set up several tests? Remember: the indicator can be rather slow to act.
- How can you make sure your tests are fair?
- What measurements will you need to make?
- How will you record your results?

What to do
- Plan your investigation.
- Ask your teacher to check your plan.
- Carry out your investigation and record all your results.
- Write a letter to the caretaker telling him what you found.
- Is there any way in which your tests could have been improved?

Disinfectant might remove mould like this

Did you know?

Not all moulds are bad for you. Cheeses like gorgonzola have to go mouldy to produce a strong flavour.

Some people were asked to think of things that make people ill. This is what they said:

1 With your group find five more things the people could have said about illness.

Here is some information about diseases:

Some diseases are caused by microbes. Doctors call these diseases **infections**. They can be passed from one person to another. Microbes which cause diseases are known as **germs**.

Food poisoning is caused by bacteria. These microbes are carried into your body on the food you eat. Diseases like whooping cough and pneumonia are caused by bacteria which get into your lungs. Doctors can treat some infections by giving you **antibiotics** to kill off the bacteria.

Flu, colds, chicken pox and measles are all caused by microbes called **viruses**. These are even smaller than bacteria. When you catch a cold, viruses get into your nose and throat and make your body produce more viruses.

Microbes can get into the body through the mouth and the nose. Some can enter the body through the skin and through cuts.

Your body has its own defence system. It gets to work whenever disease attacks. Good diet, exercise and plenty of rest all help the body defend itself against disease. Heavy smoking, a poor diet and drug-taking all make it more difficult for your body to fight disease.

People can be injected to protect them against some viruses. This is called **vaccination**. Antibiotics don't have any effect on viruses.

Give some examples of
2 diseases which can be passed on from one person to another.
3 things people can do in their lives which make it more difficult for their bodies to fight disease.
4 illnesses which are caused by microbes.

Track the infection

Some people in Easthampton have picked up an infection. It isn't serious, but it is giving them sore patches on their feet. Dr Stockton thinks that the microbes causing it are tiny bits called **spores** from a fungus. She suspects that water in a sports club changing room might be the source of the infection. But there are seven sports clubs in town. She needs someone to check some water samples to find out which changing room the microbes have come from.

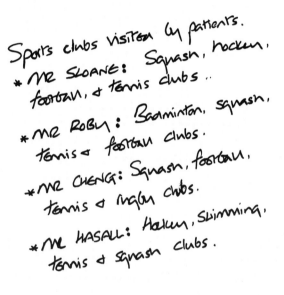

Spores seen through a microscope

Investigate

Find out which changing room is the source of the infection.

You need
Samples of water from the changing rooms, microscope, pipette, microscope slides.

Useful information
- Dr Stockton has treated the samples you are testing. Any spores in them are now completely harmless!
- The picture shows some spores under a microscope.

Things to think about
- Dr Stockton has written down details of the sports clubs visited by her patients. Do you need to check samples from *all* the changing rooms? Can you rule some of them out?

What to do
- Plan your investigation.
- Carry our your investigation.
- Record your results.
- Write a letter to Dr Stockton telling her what you found.

Sports clubs visited by patients.
* MR SLOANE: Squash, hockey, football, & tennis clubs.
* MR ROBY: Badminton, squash, tennis & football clubs.
* MR CHENG: Squash, football, tennis & rugby clubs.
* MR HASALL: Hockey, swimming, tennis & squash clubs.

Germs can be carried by the thousands of tiny droplets shot out when someone sneezes

Did you know?

Explorers once thought that the pyramids had a curse upon them. They called it the Curse of the Pharoahs. Anyone who broke the seal on a burial chamber and went inside would die! Some explorers did die, but probably not because of a curse. Spores from fungi in the sealed chambers caused a fatal lung infection. Explorers breathed in the spores when they opened the chambers.

61

Armies of harmful microbes are standing in your way. You have to battle through them. Here is a game you can play with your friends. But first you have to make the game.

You need
- Dice (you can roll a flat-sided pencil marked with the numbers 1 to 6 instead)
- 6 microbe counters for each player. You can make these out of card. Put your initials on them or colour them so that you know who they belong to.
- Game board. Copy out the one shown on the opposite page but make it at least twice as big!
- 'Where to move' instructions. Copy these out and complete them by writing ON or BACK in each blank space. You have to decide with your group which is the more suitable. For example, if you think that cleaning your teeth helps you forward in your battle against harmful microbes then complete the instruction for square 7 like this:

7 Teeth cleaned   <u>ON</u>   3 squares

The object of the game
To get all six of your counters to square 25. The first person to do this is the winner.

How to play
- Take it in turns to have your go.
- Put one of your counters on square 1. Roll the dice. Move your counter forward that number of squares.
- When you land on a number, see if there is a 'Where to move' instruction. If it says 'ON 3 squares' then move your counter on an extra three squares. If it says 'BACK 3 squares' then move your counter back three squares.
- When you reach square 25, put your counter aside and save it. Any throw that takes you past square 25 will do. When it is your turn again, start at square 1 with your next counter . . . and so on.

Where to move
These instructions tell you where to move if you land on a particular square. Copy, and complete them by writing ON or BACK in each blank space.

Square		
1	Start here	
3	Hands washed before meal	...... 3 squares
5	No baths for a month	...... 3 squares
7	Teeth cleaned	...... 3 squares
9	Food not properly cooked	...... 3 squares
11	Toilet disinfected	...... 3 squares
13	Someone sneezes nearby	...... 3 squares
15	Body vaccinated	...... 3 squares
17	Friend has 'flu	...... 3 squares
19	Meat left out of 'fridge	...... 3 squares
21	Antibiotics taken	...... 3 squares
23	Dirty knives and forks	...... 3 squares
25	Next counter!	

Squares **2, 4, 6, 8, 10, 12, 14, 16, 18, 20, 22, 24:** stay where you are until your next turn.

1	2	3	4	5
16	17	18	19	6
15	24	25	20	7
14	23	22	21	8
13	12	11	10	9

copy this board for your game

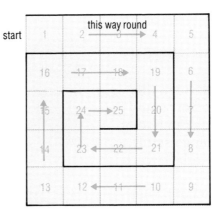

start

Healthy or not?

Look at the picture. The people are doing lots of different things.

1 Make a list of all the things which will help people stay healthy.

2 Make a list of all the things which might make people unhealthy.

Stepping stones

Helpful or harmful?

There are many types of microbes. Some of them do useful jobs for us but others are harmful.

1. Look back through this module. See how many examples you can find of microbes doing useful jobs and microbes which are harmful.
2. Make a leaflet or poster called 'Helpful and harmful microbes'. Start by describing what microbes are.

Milk microbes

3. What does the dairy do to kill off microbes in your daily milk?
4. Why do you think dried milk lasts a lot longer than fresh milk?
5. Why is fresh milk kept in a 'fridge?
6. Some microbes in milk can be very useful. What can they be used to make?
7. There are many different types of milk on sale in a supermarket. Do a survey of all the different ways you can buy milk. Look at the 'best before' and 'sell by' dates to find out how long they all keep. Make a poster to display what you have found.

Slash and burn

Slash and burn is a type of agriculture used in some forest areas. The forest is cleared of trees, which are then burnt. The ash and decayed leaves put enough nutrients in the soil for two crops to be grown one after another. After this, the soil has few nutrients left. More forest must then be cleared to grow further crops. The forest may never regrow.

8. What are the problems with this form of agriculture?
9. Find out some reasons why people are so worried about forests being cut down.

Keyword

10. Copy out the grid below. Fill in the rows with the answers to the following clues.
    1. Instrument used for looking at microbes.
    2. Smallest type of microbe.
    3. Microbes that make milk go bad.
    4. He invented a way of keeping milk drinkable.
    5. Made from grass cuttings and garden rubbish.
    6. Drink made from barley using microbes.
    7. Microbes used in making wine and beer.
    8. Food made from milk by 3 across.
11. What is the keyword down the numbered squares?

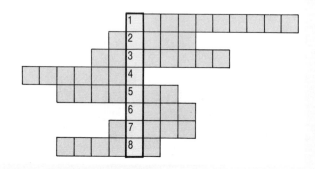

Plastic apples

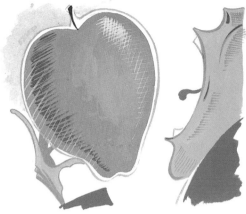

Research workers at a plastics factory have developed a new material which they claim is harmless to humans. When apples are dipped in the plastic, they are coated and keep for about five times as long as uncovered apples. This was discovered by accident when someone dropped an apple into the plastic. The apples need no other treatment; their surfaces don't need disinfecting. They are popular with some people because they have a nice glossy surface.

12 Think of a name for the new plastic.
13 Produce a poster advertising the advantages of your new treatment.
14 Would *you* eat apples covered in the new plastic? Give reasons for your answer.

Fit and healthy

Exercise helps to keep you healthy.
15 Give *five* other things people can do to help keep themselves healthy.
16 Give *five* things people should avoid doing they want to keep as healthy as possible.

Microbe multiplication

Here are some figures about the numbers of bacteria counted over an eight hour period:

Hours	Number of bacteria
0	500
1	750
2	1200
4	9000
6	1000000
8	100000000

17 Use these figures to draw a graph.
18 What would happen if microbes multiplied like this in a chicken a few hours before you ate it?
19 Some foods have to be cooked before you can eat them. What does cooking do to the microbes?
20 Why must we be careful when handling cooked and uncooked food together?

London, 1665

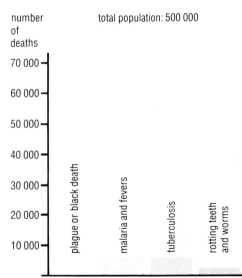

Look at this chart. It shows the main causes of death in one year (1665) in London.
21 The plague was an infectious disease. What does this mean?
22 What was London like in 1665?
23 Why did so many people die?
24 Are any of these diseases common today? If not, see if you can find out why.

OXFORD
SCIENCE
programme

C Materials and mixtures

C1.1 Building materials

The pictures show houses from around the world. The houses have been built using different materials. Some of the materials occur naturally, such as wood. Others are **synthetic**: they are made in factories using chemicals. Answer these with your group:

For each house, describe:

1. where the house has been built.
2. how old the house is.
3. what materials have been used to build the house.
4. why you think those materials have been used.
5. whether the materials are natural or synthetic.
6. whether anything has happened to the materials: for example, have they changed colour or worn away?
7. Make a poster to show your ideas about all of the houses.

A

B

C

D

E

Building work

The pictures show some building work in progress. You should be able to find:
 a window being installed
 insulating materials being placed in the walls of a house
 a beam to support the walls and roof which will go above it.
 a roof being added to a house
 a road being laid

For each of these:
8 describe the materials being used.

The material used for a window pane has to be **transparent** (see-through), and it needs to be **rigid**, not bendy. These are **properties** of the material.
9 What properties do you think the other materials you found in the pictures should each have?

Sorting them out

There are lots of different materials on these two pages. With your group:
10 Make a list of the materials.
11 Try to put the materials into groups. For example you could put them into *two* groups: natural and synthetic.
12 See how many ways you can find of putting the materials into groups. You can put them into more than two groups if you want to.

What, where and why?

Your clothes, your sports equipment and your bicycle are all made of materials. The bicycle frame is made of steel. The steel has paint on it. Where the paint has been scratched off, there may be rust. That's three materials just in the frame!

Investigate

Carry out a survey of everyday materials.

What to do
 Look around your house, in school, in the garden and other places. Make a list of all the materials you can find.
 For each material, find out:
  what it has been used for.
  whether anything has happened to the material; for example, has it changed shape or colour, or been worn away or damaged?
 Make a poster to present your results.

Scientists have a word for putting things into groups. They call it **classification**.

C1.2 Inside and outside

With your group, look at the picture of the kitchen.

1 For *each* of the following, list the *five* most important things about the material used to make it:
kitchen worktop
sink
floor covering
washing up bowl
a dish to be used in the oven
saucepans
table mats

Can you imagine . . . ?

Imagine you are the material used to make each of these:
A dish that can be used in an oven, in a microwave oven and put in the freezer.
The kitchen sink waste pipe.
The kitchen floor covering.

2 For each one, describe what happens to you during a typical day.

3 How many can you list?
4 How many different materials can you find in your kitchen?

Keeping in the heat

Donna is describing different materials. She writes:

> Materials that do not let heat through are called insulators. These Materials have lots of different Uses. In the kitchen, they are used in the cooker and the fridge. In the cooker, they stop the heat getting out. In the fridge, they stop heat getting in.
>
> They are also used in the walls of houses to stop heat escaping. This saves Money on heating bills.
>
> Warm clothes for winter also need Materials that are good insulators. People Who walk or climb in the Mountains need special clothes. It is also important for old people to Wear Warm clothes in the Winter.

5 What does Donna mean by an 'insulator'?

6 Donna gives several examples of where insulators are needed. Suggest a material that could be used for each one.

Warm clothing

When it is cold, everyone needs warm clothing. But for some people, it is especially important. To find out why, read the information on hypothermia and windchill on the right.

Investigate

Test some materials to see if they are suitable for winter clothing.

Things to think about
- What materials will you test?
- How can you test your materials to see how well they insulate? Will you need to wrap them round something warm? How will you tell how warm it is?
- When comparing different materials, how can you make sure that your tests are fair?
- Will your materials still be good insulators when they are wet or when it is windy? How can you find out?
- How will you record your results?

You need
Materials to test, items chosen by you.

What to do
- Plan your investigations.
- Make a list of the things you need.
- Ask your teacher to check your plan.
- Carry out your tests and record your results.
- Present your results.
- Make an advice leaflet for old people. This should tell them how to keep warm in the winter.

Hypothermia
Hypothermia is often called 'exposure'. It is what happens if your body gets too cold. It can affect climbers and hill walkers. And it can affect old people and young babies in the winter. Outdoors, hypothermia occurs when it is cold, wet and windy. To prevent hypothermia you must wear clothes which keep you warm and dry, and are windproof. Indoors, hypothermia can happen if people do not eat properly and the heating is poor. Every year in Britain, about 40 000 more elderly people die in the winter than in the summer. And about 20 people die of exposure on the moors and mountains.

Windchill
The wind can make it feel much colder than it is. This is because the wind takes extra heat from your body. If the wind speed is 15 mph at 0°C, the temperature feels 10°C lower. This is sometimes called the *windchill* factor. In hills and mountains, the chilling effect of the wind can be even more.

C1.3 Holding things up

These photographs show some structures. Structures are designed to take loads. Answer these with your group:

1 What is the load on each of these structures?
2 Is anything happening to each structure because of its load? If so, what?

A load is a type of force.

3 Make up *five* sentences including the word 'force'.
4 Look at the sentences other people have produced. Sort out the best five ideas. Put these onto a poster called 'Our ideas about forces'.

You use forces every day. You use a force to open a door. You use a force to stop your bike. A force keeps you on the ground.

5 Make a list of the forces you use or feel. For each one, say what is producing the force.

Some forces are useful, but others are not. In your list of forces:

6 Which forces are useful?
7 Which cause problems?
8 Can any of these problems be overcome? If so, how?

A mystery force

'May the force be with you'. This was said in a famous science fiction film.

9 What do you think it means? Do you think this is a correct use of the word force?

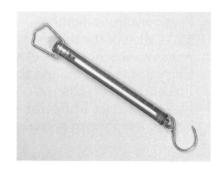

Looking into springs

Forces make springs stretch. Perhaps the idea could be used to measure forces!

Investigate

- Find out how a spring stretches by hanging weights on it. The diagrams on the right show you how to carry out the investigation.
- Repeat your investigations with different springs.
- What do your results tell you?

Measuring forces

You can measure forces using a **newtonmeter** like the one in the picture below left. It has a spring inside, and a scale on it marked in **newtons**, or **N** for short. The newton is the unit scientists use for measuring force.

Investigate

- Try to estimate some of the 'everyday forces' you listed earlier like turning a door handle.
- Use a newtonmeter to measure the forces.
- Draw a table to record your results. How close were your estimates?

Testing materials

You can find out how strong different materials are by seeing what happens to them when they have forces on them.

Investigate

Test some materials to find the answers to these questions:
- Do the materials all stretch evenly like a spring?
- Do they go back to the length they started if you take the force away?
- What is the largest force they can take before breaking?

You need
Materials to test, such as wires and threads.

What to do
- Plan your investigations. Decide what materials you will test.
- Ask your teacher to check that your investigations are safe.
- Carry out your investigations and record your results.
- What did you discover from your results?

Did you know?

The newton was named after Sir Isaac Newton, a famous scientist who lived about 300 years ago.

10 See what you can find out about Sir Isaac Newton.

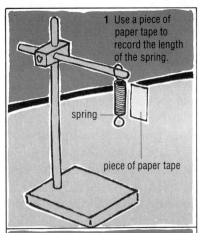

1 Use a piece of paper tape to record the length of the spring.

spring

piece of paper tape

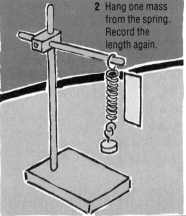

2 Hang one mass from the spring. Record the length again.

3 Add more masses, one at a time. Record the length each time.

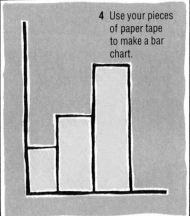

4 Use your pieces of paper tape to make a bar chart.

C1.4 The gardener's problem

Dave is a keen gardener. He needs somewhere to grow his seeds and to protect his plants in the winter. But he does not have enough space to build a greenhouse. He decides to design and make something himself. You can see his design in the picture. The frame is going to be made of wood. But Dave can't decide what material to use for the lid. After visiting his local hardware shop and garden centre he finds that there are three materials that he could use:
  glass
  clear plastic
  thin flexible polythene
    sheet

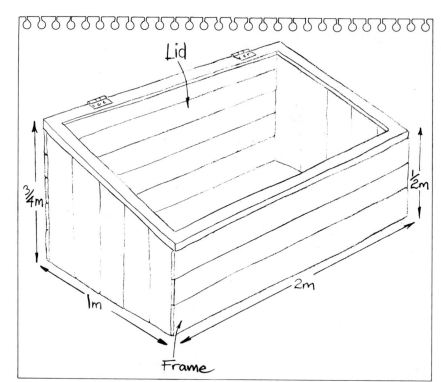

See if you can help Dave make a choice. Start by thinking about the properties different materials can have. There is a list on the right to help you. Look at the list:
1 Explain what each property on the list means.
2 For each one, give an example of material with that property.

Now decide what a good lid should do.
3 Write down all the things which the lid has to do.
4 From the list of properties, choose the ones which are needed for the lid material. Are there any other things to think about which are not on the list? Write these down.

You have now listed all the properties which the lid material should have. A list like this is called a **specification**. The cost of the material could also be very important.
5 Try to find out the cost of the three materials.

Describing materials:
  strong
  hard
  tough
  rigid
  flexible
  transparent (see through)
  opaque (*not* see through)
  high melting point
  heat insulator
  shatterproof
  easy to cut and drill

Help for the gardener

To help Dave, you must try to find out which of the three materials is the best – glass, clear plastic or polythene sheet. For a big investigation like this, it would be useful to work with a team. The pictures on the right might help you plan and carry out your work together.

Investigate

Investigate the properties of glass, clear plastic and polythene sheeting. Find out which material would be best for Dave's lid. You don't need to make a full-size greenhouse!

You need
Glass, clear plastic, polythene sheeting, items chosen by you.

Things to think about
- Which properties will you need to investigate?
- How will you share out the work? Would it be best to investigate one property each?
- In your investigation, how will you compare the materials?
- How can you make sure that your tests are fair?
- What measurements will you need to make?
- How will you make these measurements?
- How will you record your results?

What to do
Planning and designing:
- Plan your investigations. Decide who does what.
- Draw labelled sketches of your ideas.
- Make a list of all the equipment you need.
- Ask your teacher to check that your investigations are safe.

Testing:
- Carry out your investigations.
- Record your results.

Presenting:
- Put all the team's results together.
- Find an attractive and interesting way to present the results.
- Write a letter to Dave telling him everything you found.

Evaluating:
You need to find out how well your work went. You need to **evaluate** your work:
- Check your specification.
- Check your solution against the problem. Did you solve Dave's problem?
- Did things happen the way you expected?
- If you did the investigation again, what would you do differently?
- What have you learnt from the investigation?
- Did your team work well together?

Designing and planning

Testing

Presenting

Evaluating

C2.1 Solids, liquids and gases

What am I?

I am white and fluffy and the children play with me in the garden. Some grown-ups are spoil sports and throw salt at me to try to make me go away. When the sun shines strongly I warm up and run to the lowest part of the garden. If I am feeling really energetic, I may leave the path altogether and take to the skies!

The answer to this riddle is snow. What clues tell you when the riddle is referring to:

1. a **solid** (the snow)?
2. a **liquid** (the puddle, when the snow had melted)?
3. a **gas** (when the water from the puddle had **evaporated** to become invisible **water vapour** in the air)?

Look at the examples of different substances on the right. Some of these are solids, some liquids and some gases.

4. What do you think each one is? Make a table to show your ideas.
5. With your group, make up some useful rules which could help someone to pick out the solids. Then do the same for the liquids and the gases.

Scientists call solids, liquids and gases the three **states** of matter. Each state has got its own special **properties** (ways of behaving).

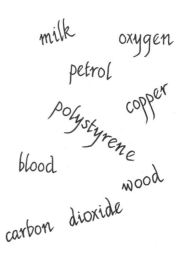

milk oxygen petrol copper polystyrene blood wood carbon dioxide

What's happening here?

When snow melts, a solid (ice) changes its state to becomes a liquid (water). What change of state is taking place in each of the pictures below?

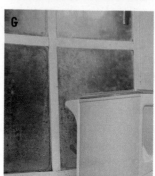

Melting and freezing

Investigate

Ice melts at 0°C. Water freezes at 0°C.
Find out if both of these statements can be true.

You need
Boiling tube, crushed ice, thermometer, beaker, freezing mixture, cold water, warm water.

What to do
- Try both of the experiments in the diagrams.
- What makes the water in the boiling tube cool down?
- What makes the ice in the boiling tube warm up?
- At what temperature does the water freeze?
- At what temperature does the ice melt?
- From your observations, is it possible to have water *and* ice at 0°C?

Quiz game

6 Try this quiz game with a partner. It will help you to recognize some of the special properties of solids, liquids and gases.

First player   Choose the name of a substance from the table you wrote out before. Your partner will be trying to work out whether you have picked a solid, a liquid or a gas. She or he will be asking you up to ten questions. But don't give away too much information!

Second player   Your partner will choose a substance from his or her table. You can ask up to ten questions to find out whether it is a solid, a liquid or a gas.

7 After a few tries each, stop the quiz. Decide which questions were most useful when trying to identify the solids, liquids and gases.

More evaporation

Many shops and cafes provide air driers instead of towels for drying your hands. The stream of warm air produced by the drier helps the water on your hands evaporate quickly. When the water evaporates, it turns into a gas (water vapour) without actually boiling. Your hands may be warmed a bit by the dryer but they will be a lot cooler than boiling water!

8 Make a list of some other examples of the evaporation of water and other liquids.

9 Design an experiment to find out more about the ways in which evaporation can be speeded up.

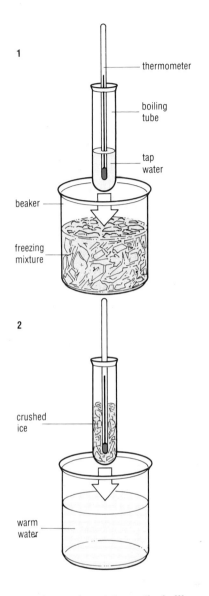

In each experiment, lower the boiling tube into the beaker, watch carefully and write down your observations.

Changing liquid into gas

C2.2   Mass and volume

In shops, laboratories, hospitals and factories, people often have to measure things.

Little and large masses

In school science labs, we usually measure the mass of things in **grams** (**g** for short). Sometimes if the mass is large, we work in **kilograms** (**kg** for short). There are 1000 grams in one kilogram. Very small quantities are measured in **milligrams** but you don't usually use such small amounts in school experiments. There are 1000 milligrams in a gram.

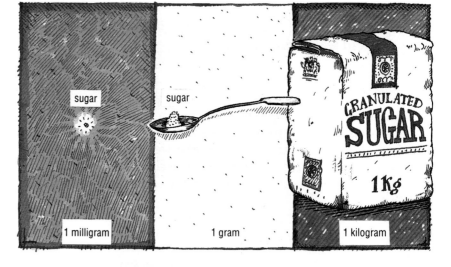

How accurate?

Often in everyday life we are quite happy to use approximate quantities, like a 'pinch' of salt or a 'spoonful' of sugar. Sometimes this is also true in science. At other times, we have to be as accurate as possible.

Not very accurate

Accurate

Little and large volumes

In shops, liquid products are usually sold by volume. The bottles are marked in **litres** (**l**), or in **millilitres** (**ml**) for smaller quantities. One millilitre takes up the same volume as a cube with sides of one centimetre. In science, we often call this volume a **centimetre cubed** (written **cm³** for short) instead of a millilitre.

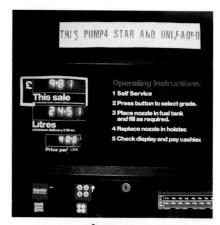

Accurate

1 Check the containers in your laboratory. What units are marked on them?

Pair them up

2 Look at the jumbled up items below. Decide which ones go best together and pair them up.

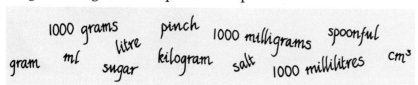

Who's been eating my Krispies?

The Bear family have found that their new packet of Krispies isn't full. They think they've been visited by the Krispie thief! On the side of the packet, it says: 'This product is packed by mass, not volume. Contents may settle during transit.'

Investigate

Find out what might have happened to the Krispies.

You need
Krispies, measuring cylinder, mass balance.

What to do
- Pour a portion of Krispies into a measuring cylinder.
- Measure the mass of the Krispies.
- Measure the volume taken up by the Krispies.
- Gently shake the cylinder from side to side for 15 seconds. Now measure the mass and the volume again.
- What has happened to the mass of the Krispies?
- What has happened to the volume taken up by the Krispies?
- How would you explain to the Bear family that they have probably not been visited by the Krispie thief?

From the supermarket

The products in the picture were all bought in a supermarket:

3 Which products would you expect to be sold by volume and which by mass?
4 Which products would you expect to settle during transit like the Krispies?

Check the label

The label in the picture is on a bottle of cough medicine.
5 Why is it important to shake the contents of the bottle thoroughly before pouring out the medicine?
6 Why do you think the recommended dosage of medicine increases with the age of the patient?
7 From the dosage suggested, what do you think would be a suitable quantity of medicine for a man of average height and mass?

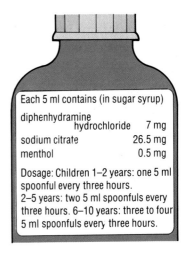

Each 5 ml contains (in sugar syrup)

diphenhydramine hydrochloride	7 mg
sodium citrate	26.5 mg
menthol	0.5 mg

Dosage: Children 1–2 years: one 5 ml spoonful every three hours.
2–5 years: two 5 ml spoonfuls every three hours. 6–10 years: three to four 5 ml spoonfuls every three hours.

This medicine is not normally sold for adults. Instead, a 'stronger' medicine with the same ingredients is available. Two 5 ml spoonfuls of this is recommended for the average adult.
8 In what ways do you think the medicines might be the same?
9 In what ways do you think the medicines might be different?

C2.3   Dissolving things

Lots of things **dissolve** in water. This makes it a very useful substance. For example, salt dissolves in water. Scientists say that salt is **soluble** in water, and that water is the **solvent**. Once the salt has dissolved, the liquid you have is a **solution** of salt and water. In the picture, there are some more examples of substances that dissolve in water.

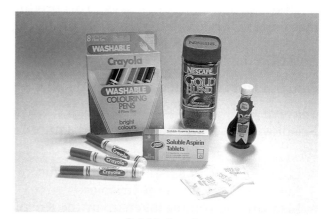

Soluble in water

1 What do the four words written in darker letters in the sentences above mean?
2 The substances in the picture are specially made to be soluble in water. Explain why each one needs to be soluble.

Dissolving sugar

Fred, Jo and Sharon are having a tea break together. They all take one lump of sugar in their tea but only Jo takes milk.
3 Work out what each person likes to put in their tea.
4 Would you expect each person's sugar to dissolve in the same time?

Investigate

Compare the ways in which the friends make their drinks. Find a way of measuring how long it takes the sugar to dissolve in each case.

You need
Sugar lumps, clock or stopwatch, items chosen by you.

What to do
- Plan your investigation and list the equipment you need.
- Carry out your investigation. What did you find?
- When Fred is washing up, he finds some sugar in the bottom of Jo's mug. What reasons could there be for this?
- Think of a simple way of making sure that all Jo's sugar dissolves next time. Change your experiment to check this.

Solutions around the house

Oil, tar and grass stains are difficult to remove from your skin by washing in water. Ordinary soap helps, but special mixtures of chemicals such as Swarfega work much better. Many shops sell products to remove stains from fabrics. The picture shows one example.
5 Why can chemicals like Swarfega remove stains?
6 Find out what other products you can buy for removing stains and what they each remove.

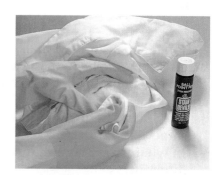

Treating a ball-point pen stain with a liquid called diethylene glycol

Dissolved gases

You have seen that some solids dissolve in water. Some gases do as well. In a fish tank, the water plants produce oxygen. Some of this oxygen dissolves in water. The fish need the dissolved oxygen to survive. They take it in through their gills.

7 Some fish tanks have air pumps fitted. Why do you think this is?

The water in this fish tank has oxygen dissolved in it

How about a drink?

How about a solution of carbonated water with a little dissolved sugar, citric acid and sodium citrate? If you don't like the sound of that, how about some lemonade. It's the same thing! 'Carbonated water' is another way of saying water with carbon dioxide gas dissolved in it. Carbon dioxide gives the drink its fizz. You can see bubbles of carbon dioxide rising out of the drink when you take the top off the bottle.

Investigate

Find out how much carbon dioxide you swallow every time you have a drink of lemonade, carbonated water or some other fizzy drink.

You need
Fizzy drink (carbonated water is a good one to use because it is not sticky), items chosen by you.

Useful information
- Carbon dioxide is a colourless gas, so you can't see it.
- Carbon dioxide sinks downwards in air.

Things to think about
- How will you trap and collect the carbon dioxide from the drink?
- How can you be certain that you are collecting *only* carbon dioxide?
- How will you measure the carbon dioxide you collect. Will it be easier to measure the mass or the volume of the gas?

What to do
- Plan your investigation.
- Make a list of the equipment you need.
- Ask your teacher to check your plan.
- Carry out your investigation.
- How much carbon dioxide was dissolved in the drink?

C2.4 Sweet business

Kevin has decided to raise money for charity by making and selling caramel squares. He has found a recipe but he is having trouble understanding some of the instructions. See if you can help him.

1 What equipment will Kevin need for measuring out the ingredients?

2 What will happen to the ingredients as they are slowly heated and stirred?

3 How will Kevin be able to tell that the contents of the saucepan have 'come to the boil'?

4 Why do you think that it is important to stir the mixture continuously when it has reached its boiling temperature?

When Kevin has made the caramel he pours it into a baking tray. Later, when the caramel is cool, he cuts it into squares and lifts one out to eat.

5 What does this tell you about the way in which the caramel has changed as it has cooled?

Meanwhile, in a biscuit factory . . .

The biscuit in the pictures below is made in a factory. It has a toffee filling, made from similar ingredients to Kevin's caramel squares. The toffee is poured onto the biscuit base and then the whole lot is covered in a layer of chocolate. Each biscuit is wrapped in a sealed wrapper. Then lots of biscuits are packed together in boxes ready for the shops.

Lorries bring the ingredients to the factory in huge quantities. More lorries take the finished biscuit to warehouses ready for delivery to shops and supermarkets.

Caramel squares

1 tin of condensed milk

50ml (3 tablesp.) golden syrup

150g block margarine

150g granulated sugar

Method
Place the condensed milk, golden syrup and margarine in a saucepan and heat gently, stirring frequently until all the margarine has melted. Add the sugar and continue heating gently, stirring frequently until all the sugar has melted. Bring the mixture to the boil, stirring continuously. Continue boiling for 5 minutes.

This biscuit is shown actual size. Its mass is 20 grams.

6 How many biscuits will fit in a box 30 cm long by 20 cm wide by 10 cm deep?

7 What is the total mass of these biscuits in *grams*? What is it in *kilograms*?

There is a plan of a biscuit factory on the right. It shows the main areas where biscuit production takes place. The photographs below show some of the stages in the production of biscuits.

8 Describe how you think the factory would produce the biscuits. Use a flow chart if you wish. Start from the delivery bay where the tankers and lorries arrive with ingredients. Describe all the stages until the finished biscuits are wrapped, boxed and ready for sending to customers.

9 Many of the processes need specially designed machines. Why is this?

10 Are there any stages where you think that people can do a better job than machines?

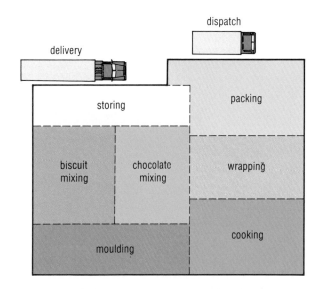

Mixing the ingredients

Coating the biscuits

Wrapping the biscuits

All the money Kevin got by selling his caramel squares was profit for the charity. Kevin didn't have to be paid. And his family donated the ingredients, the cooking costs and even the washing-up liquid for cleaning up afterwards! However, in the biscuit factory everything has to be paid for.

11 Make a list of all the things that cost money during the making, packaging and selling of biscuits from the factory.

12 Invent your own variety of biscuit. Use drawings and flow charts to describe how your biscuit would be manufactured. Choose a name for your biscuit and describe how you would advertise it.

C3.1 Sludge, steam and blots

Answer these with your group, then swap your ideas with other groups:

In our homes, there is a lot of waste stuff to get rid of.

1 Make a list of all the waste things that you need to get rid of from a house.

2 Which of these things are carried away by pipes?

Plenty of waste things go down the sink:

3 Make a list of things which go down the sink.

4 Do you think each of these things is pure or impure?

5 Where do all these waste things go?

6 Why are these waste things separated?

7 How are they separated?

8 What happens to the different parts after separation?

Wet clothes or dry clothes?

Clothes will dry if it is not raining.

9 How do they dry?

10 A windy day is a better day for drying than a calm day. Why?

11 A sunny day is better for drying than a cloudy day. Why?

A steaming time!

Condensation which forms on cold windows is only pure water.

12 Why does the water collect on the windows?

13 How does it get to the window?

14 What is happening in the saucepan?

Ink blots

It is difficult writing on tissue paper with a felt-tip pen. It's even more difficult if the paper is wet.

Investigate

Find out what happens to an ink blot on a piece of filter paper when water is added to it.

You need
Felt-tip pens, filter paper, beaker of water, pipette to drop water, beaker or board to support filter paper.

What to do
- Use a felt-tip pen to put an ink blot in the centre of a piece of filter paper. The blot should not be more than 5 mm across.
- Drop water, one drop at a time, onto the ink blot. Allow each drop to be soaked up before you add the next one.
- What happens to the ink blot? Keep a record of all your findings.
- What has happened to the dyes which make up the coloured ink?
- Try some other pens and see what happens. You could try different makes of the same colour pen.
- Make a poster display of your findings. What did you find out about the coloured dyes in pens?

water in pipette

filter paper

ink blot

C3.2   Clean up

The newspaper report describes a disaster off the South East coast.

1 What damage do you think might be caused by such a disaster?

Exploring the oil damage

You have to check whether the coastline has been polluted. Samples from the coastline have been taken by a scientist like the person in the picture. She has taken two samples. One is from the surface of the river estuary where she was working. This sample may contain oil with salt water. The other was from the same place, but from the bottom of the river estuary. This sample contains mud with salt water.

Investigate

Separate out the oil, salt, mud and sand from two samples of estuary water.

Before you carry out your investigation, you will need to know about filtering, evaporating, decanting and distilling.

▪ Practise each of these processes before you start.

You need
Two samples of estuary water, items chosen by you.

Things to think about
● Which substance will you separate first?

What to do
▪ Plan your investigation and list all the equipment you need.
▪ Ask your teacher to check your plan.
▪ Carry out your investigations and decide whether your samples were polluted.
▪ *Keep any mud and water you separate out.* You will need them for investigations on the next spread.
▪ Could your methods be improved in any way? If so, how?
▪ Present your results so that others can find out what you discovered.

Collision causes oil slick off Southend

Just after midnight last night a 50,000 ton oil tanker signalled for help off the south east coast

A 5000 ton cargo vessel had rammed the oil tanker half way down its port side. The Captain reported that he was losing oil but that his ship was not in immediate danger of sinking.

Rescue craft arrived within two hours and are still working at the scene of the disaster. So far they have been unable to stop the loss of oil from the tanker and a huge slick is forming. Weather reports suggest that the oil slick will head straight for the coast. Environmental groups were reported to be very concerned about the effects of the oil on wildlife. They were preparing for the worst. Government experts reported that all efforts were being made

Testing the water

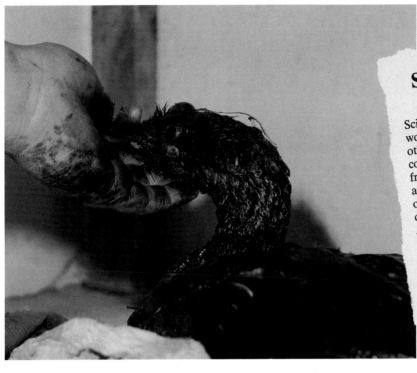

Slick crisis worsens

Scientists are becoming increasingly worried about the threat to birds and other wildlife along the South East coast. After last week's oil leakage from a tanker off Southend, large amounts of oil have been washed up on shore. At the last report some 5000 dead birds have been collected. Another 2000 have been treated. One scientist commented, 'Oil pollution clogs up the feathers of birds. This stops them from escaping from the slick once they are in it. Often the birds swallow the oil and this poisons them.'

Imagine that you are a bird caught in an oil slick.

2 What would it feel like?
3 How would you try to get out?
4 What problems would you have?
5 Who might rescue you?

You could answer these questions by writing a story, poem or play which you can share with other groups.

Oily feathers

Crude oil in the feathers of birds causes them lots of problems. If the birds are to be helped, this oil has to be removed from the feathers. Often the cure also takes out other oils. These are naturally on the bird's feathers. Without these oils the feathers do not work properly.

Investigate

There are a number of feathers from birds available. Some of them have been polluted with oil, some have not. Find a way of getting the oil out of the polluted feathers. Then compare your treated feathers with the unpolluted feathers and decide whether your treatment could be safely used to treat birds polluted with oil.

You need
Polluted feathers, unpolluted feathers, items chosen by you.

Things to think about
- What methods will you try for removing the oil?
- Will your methods damage the feathers?
- How will you tell if the treatment has been successful?
- Feathers need to move air. They also need to be waterproof. Will the treated feathers still be able to do their job properly?

What to do
- Plan your investigation.
- Make a list of the things you need. Discuss these with your teacher.
- Try out your treatments.
- Have you managed to clean the feathers?
- Do you think that your method could be used on birds? Give some reasons.
- How could your methods be improved?
- Make a display of your work. Make sure that you show your treated and untreated feathers.

C3.3   Pure or impure?

Just because something is unpolluted it doesn't mean that it is pure. Polluted sea water isn't pure. But sea water on its own isn't pure either! Something is only pure if it is just one substance by itself. Anything added to a pure substance is called an **impurity**. If you add salt to pure water the salt is an impurity.

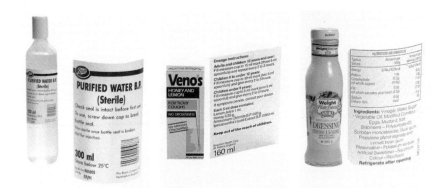

1 Why is sea water not pure?
2 Decide whether each of the things in the picture is pure or not.

Safe to drink?

In the table on the right, Data A shows you the maximum amounts of some impurities which are allowed in tap water. Data B shows you the actual amounts of impurities which were found in a sample of tap water.

Are these substances pure or not?

Substances (impurities)	Mass in milligrams in every litre of tap water	
	Data A maximum allowed	Data B sample of tap water
Sulphates	250	25
Magnesium	50	30
Sodium	150	20
Potassium	12	10

3 Draw a bar chart using Data A and Data B. Design your chart so that you can compare the two sets of data easily.
4 Explain whether the tap water in Data B safe to drink?

Boiling points

Investigate

The temperature at which a liquid boils is called its boiling point. Find the boiling points of pure water and salt water and compare them.

You need
Pure water, salt water, beaker, bunsen, tripod, gauze, heatproof mat, thermometer.

What to do
- Heat each water separately until they boil.
- Record the temperature at which they boil.
- How do the boiling points compare?

One way of checking the purity of water is to see if it boils at the correct temperature (100° C). The method works with other substances as well. But it is not foolproof! The temperature at which a liquid boils changes slightly depending on conditions in the atmosphere.

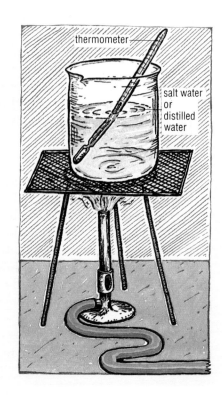

thermometer

salt water or distilled water

In an investigation on the previous spread, you had to separate out the water, mud, oil, salt and sand in two samples of estuary water. Now see if you can find out how pure the water and mud are.

How pure is the water?

Investigate

Check the purity of the water which you separated out before.

You need
Water (kept from before), beaker, bunsen, tripod, gauze, heatproof mat, thermometer.

What to do
- Find the boiling point of the water.
- Is the water pure? If not, why not?

Pure or not?

Some people say that milk, mineral water and swimming pool water are pure.
5 Do you agree with them? If not, explain why you think they are wrong.

The picture below gives you one clue. Here are two more!
- On some bottles of mineral water, the label lists the different chemicals in the water.
- Swimming pools smell of chlorine.

How pure is the mud?

Most plants can't grow in soil or mud which has large amounts of salt in it. You can use this idea to find out how pure your mud is.

Investigate

Check the purity of the mud which you separated out before.

You need
Mud (kept from before), salt-free soil, containers, seedlings.

Getting ready to plant a seedling

Things to think about
- Is it important to find out how the seedlings grow in salt-free soil? If so, why?
- How long will you leave your seedlings to grow?
- How often will you check them?
- How will you decide if the seedlings are healthy or sickly?
- How can you make sure that your tests are fair?
- How will you record any data you collect?

What to do
- Plan your investigation.
- Carry out the investigation.
- What did you find out about the mud which you separated?
- Could you improve your tests in any way? If so how?
- Produce a report about the tests on mud and water.

C3.4 Spreading out mixtures

Which pen forged the cheque?

Detectives know that a cheque has been changed. A 'y' and a '0' have been added so that eight pounds has become eighty pounds. The police think that one of four pens was used to forge the cheque. But they need to know which one.

Investigate

Find out which pen was used to forge the cheque.

You need
Suspect pens, chromatography equipment and paper, solvents.

Useful information
* Inks are a mixture of different dyes. You may already have found this out in the 'ink-blot' experiment on a previous spread.
* You can use a process called **chromatography** to separate the parts in some mixtures. The diagrams show two ways of doing chromatography. When a liquid called a **solvent** washes through the ink dots, the dyes separate out to form a pattern. The pattern on the paper is called a **chromatogram**.
* Different types of ink may need different solvents. Water is one solvent you can try. Others include ethanol, methanol and propanone. *Warning! these are toxic and inflammable.* They must not be used near a flame.

Things to think about
* Do you need to get the inks from the cheque? If so, how will you do this? If not, will you do the chromatography on the cheque itself?
* How will you decide which solvent to use?
* How will you be able to tell which pen was used?

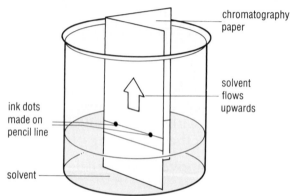

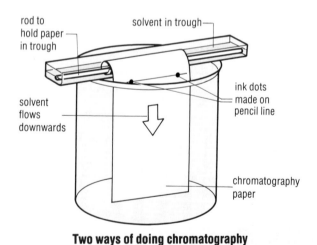

Two ways of doing chromatography

What to do
* Plan your investigation.
* Find out which pen was used for the forgery.
* Make a poster to show what you have done. On it, show your chromatograms. Say which pen you think was used in the forgery and give your reasons.

Looking for E-numbers

1 Read this short play with your group.

DAVE   My Dad says that E-numbers are bad for you. Lots of them are made using chemicals; they're artificial.

CARLA   I heard that it was the colours put in food that cause the problem. They make some people ill.

DAVE   Well, I'm going to check the sides of food packets from now on. I'm not going to eat anything with E-numbers in.

SUE   I think you are worrying too much Dave. I read the same article as Carla. It said that artificial dyes called azo dyes affect a few people, mainly those suffering from asthma or eczema ('x-ma').

CARLA   Didn't it say that the dyes were giving them skin rashes, blurred vision, and watery eyes and noses?

SUE   Yes, and all the food colourings have an E-number. It's between E100 and E199.

DAVE   I'll avoid those numbers then.

CARLA   It's not that easy Dave. You see, some of the E-numbers are natural colours. E160a is one. It's a colour found in carrots!

DAVE   I suppose I ought to find a book about food additives and read more about the subject.

The table below shows some E-number colours and the sorts of food that they are in.

2 Which E-number colours do you eat in your food?

3 Which of these colours are artificial?

Name	Colour	E-number	Artificial or natural	Examples of typical food containing these colours
Curcumin	orange	E100	Natural	Savoury rice, curry powders, margarine
Tartrazine	yellow	E102	Artificial	Sweets, chewing gum, fizzy drinks, tinned fruit, salad cream, orange and lemon squash
Sunset yellow	yellow	E110	Artificial	Sweets, packet trifle mix, apricot jam
Carmoisine	red	E122	Artificial	Packet jellies, packet soup mix, brown sauce
Calcium carbonate	white	E170	Natural	Bread, biscuits, ice cream, tablets
Beetroot red	purple-red	E162	Natural	Oxtail soup
α, β or γ carotene	orange-yellow	E160a	Natural	Soft margarine, prepacked sponge cake, yogurt, dessert whips
Annatto	yellow	E160b	Natural	Margarine, Cheshire cheese, butter, frying oil
Erythrosine	red	E127	Artificial	Glacé cherries, tinned cherries, strawberries and rhubarb, biscuits, quick custard mix

Looking for E102

People who suffer from asthma and eczema are sensitive to E102, tartrazine. So it's important to know which foods it is in.

Investigate

Use chromatography to find out whether some food colouring contains any E102.

You need
Food colouring, sample of pure tartrazine (E102) chromatography equipment.

Things to think about
- How are you going to compare the food colouring and the tartrazine?
- What type of chromatography will you do?
- Which solvent will you use?

What to do
- Plan and carry out your investigation.
- What did you discover about the food colouring? Write a report.
- How do you think you could improve your investigation?

C3.5   Unmixing mixtures

Oil companies get their oil from the ground. They call it crude oil and they collect it by drilling wells. There is a lot of crude oil in the ground under the North Sea.

Crude oil is a mixture. It isn't any use until the mixture has been separated at an oil refinery like the one in the photograph. The diagram shows you how. The crude oil is boiled. Each part of the mixture boils at a different temperature. The part which boils at the lowest temperature boils first and is collected at the top of the column. The part with the highest boiling point boils last and is collected from the bottom of the column. Separating mixtures by boiling is called **distilling**. The different parts of the mixture are called **fractions**.

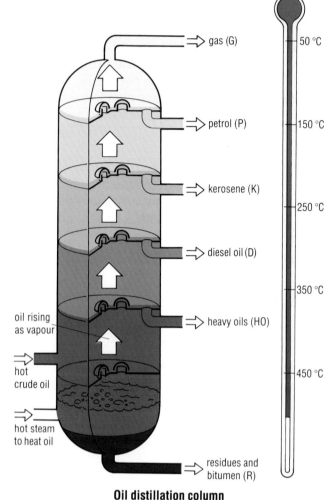

Oil distillation column

Make a poster

1 Look at the information in the diagram and in the chart. Make a poster to show how crude oil is distilled and how the different fractions from the oil can be used.

Things to think about
* Will you just copy the diagram above, or present the information in your own way?
* Can you find magazine pictures which show some of the things which are made from the fractions in oil?
* Will you find any other information about oil and put it on your poster as well?
* Do you want to deal with just one fraction or give extra information about all of them?

Uses of crude oil fractions	
Fraction	Uses (sometimes after further treatment)
G	gas fuels such as Calor gas, making other chemicals
P	fuel for cars, pesticides, drugs, plastics, fertilizers, detergents, solvents, making other chemicals
K	paraffin, jet fuel, white spirit
D	fuel for trucks and buses, central heating oil
HO	lubricating oils and grease, waxes, polishes, making other chemicals
R	tar for road surfaces, waterproof roofing materials, fuel for power stations.

Filters at work

Sieving and filtering are useful ways of separating things. But they are really the same thing! A sieve has big holes in it. Filter paper has small holes in it. The holes are so small that you can't see them.

Some people make tea by putting tea leaves straight in the pot. When they pour the tea, they use a strainer to sieve the tea leaves. Other people make tea using tea bags. In a tea bag, the tea leaves have filter paper round them. The paper is full of tiny holes which people sometimes call 'perforations'. When you add boiling water, parts of the tea leaves dissolve. This makes a solution which we call tea. The teabag filters the tea leaves. The tiny holes stop the tea leaves getting out of the bag.

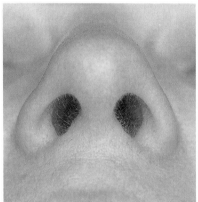

A hairy nose is a bit like a tea bag! It works as a filter. It helps stop dirt and dust entering your lungs when you breathe in. The hairs let the air through but not the dirt and dust. Believe it or not, all noses are hairy!

2 Gardeners use sieves. What do they use them for? How do they work?

3 Some people drink filter coffee. Why is it called this?

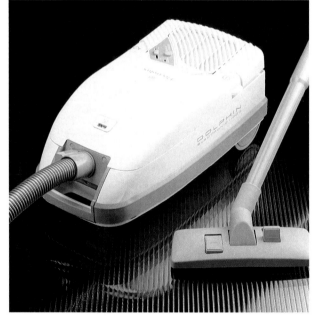

The girl in the picture is wearing nose and mouth protection.

4 How is she still able to breathe?

5 What is the nose and mouth protection doing?

6 Why do you think the hairs in the nose need extra help when wood is being sanded?

A vacuum cleaner has filter paper in it.

7 Try to find out where it is fitted and why it is needed.

8 Can you think of any other items of household equipment with a filter fitted? If so, list them.

Stepping stones

Sorting them out

There are lots of different materials mentioned in this module.

1. Go back through the module. List all the materials you come across.
2. See how many different ways you can find of putting the materials in groups. Remember, we call this **classification**.
3. Compare these with the groupings you did in C1.1.

Lost in the wash

This is the page of notes which Mark wrote about his investigations on solids, liquids and gases. Unfortunately, the page was still in his pocket when his trousers were washed.

4. Help Mark by rewriting his notes, filling in all the pieces which were lost.

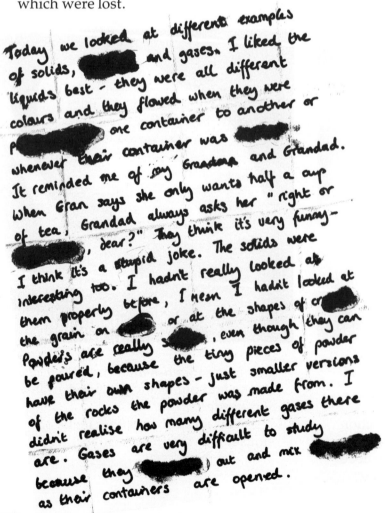

> Today we looked at different examples of solids, ███████ and gases. I liked the liquids best - they were all different colours and they flowed when they were p███████ one container to another or whenever their container was ███████ It reminded me of my Grandma and Grandad. When Gran says she only wants half a cup of tea, Grandad always asks her "right or ███████, dear?" They think it's very funny — I think it's a stupid joke. The solids were interesting too. I hadn't really looked at them properly before, I mean I hadn't looked at the grain on ███████ or at the shapes of cr███████ Powders are really s███████, even though they can be poured, because the tiny pieces of powder have their own shapes — just smaller versions of the rocks the powder was made from. I didn't realise how many different gases there are. Gases are very difficult to study because they ███████ out and mix as their containers are opened.

Words and phrases

5. For each of the following words and phrases, write a sentence describing some everyday happening which uses that word or phrase:

pour	melts
dissolves	freeze
boiling point	soluble
mass	evaporation
volume	change of state

A new material

Scientists are trying to invent a new material. It is to be used in operations for hip replacements and repairing broken bones. In the body it will have to do the same job as bone.

6. Write a full **specification** for this material. Include all the properties you think it should have.

Floaters and sinkers

Imagine that you are having trouble convincing your younger brother that ships can be made from metal. Your brother says, 'Our knives and forks are made from metal and they always sink to the bottom of the washing-up water.'

7. Plan how you could use other items usually found at home to convince your brother that metal ships do float and can carry cargo. Write down what you would say or make models to show your ideas.

How hot?

8 Estimate the temperatures of the following. Then write them down in order, starting with the hottest at the top:

Water in a swimming pool

Ice lolly

Can of Cola from the 'fridge

Warm sunny day in Britain!

Oven with a cake in it

Boiling water in a kettle

Freshly cooked chips

Bunsen flame

'Cup-a-soup'

Metal surface of an iron

South Pole at night.

Forces

A student was asked to explain forces. This is what she wrote:

> Forces can do two things. They can make something change shape or change position.

9 Explain in more detail what she meant.

Bags and strainers

sieve   ⟨⟩   filter

big holes   little holes

Think about a tea-bag and a tea strainer. In some ways they do the same job. In other ways, the things they do are different.

10 Make two lists to show these likenesses and differences.

11 What investigations could you do to find out more about the likenesses and differences?

Sweet check-up

Some sweets used to contain the yellow food colouring tartrazine, E102. Now, it should no longer be used in sweets.

12 Look at the labels on as many packets of sweets as you can. Check to see if E102 is listed on any of them.

13 How would you find out if a sweet had E102 in it?

Household purity

14 Do a survey of household things to find out how many of them are pure substances. Here are some of the things you could check: tinned foods, packet foods, kitchen and bathroom cleaners, soap powders.

15 Draw charts to show the main ingredients in different things. Can you see any patterns in what you have found?

OXFORD
SCIENCE
programme

D Living with electricity

D1.1 Charges, crackles and sparks

Defying gravity

Karen can make balloons stick to the wall by rubbing them on her jumper. You want to make balloons stick to the wall for a party. Naturally you want the balloons to stay up as long as possible. But you have no glue or string. So you have to use the same method as Karen.

Investigate

Find out the best way of making a balloon stick to the wall by rubbing.

You need
Balloon, materials for rubbing balloon.

Things to think about
- Which materials will you choose?
- Does it matter how long you rub the balloon?
- Does the shape of the balloon matter?
- Could different wall surfaces affect how long the balloon stays up?
- Will you need to measure how long the balloon stays up?
- How can you make sure that your tests are fair?
- How will you record your results?

What to do
- Plan your investigation.
- Ask your teacher to check your plan.
- Carry out your investigation.
- Record your results.
- Make a poster to show other groups what you found.
- Compare your results. Did other groups find the same as you?

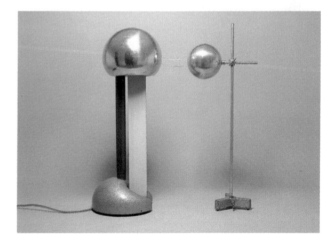

Materials to rub on a balloon:

nylon	silk	polyester
wool	linen	acetate
cotton	fur	Terylene
acrylic	paper	viscose

Charging by friction

Scientists think that a balloon picks up an **electric charge** when it is rubbed on a jumper. They call this charging by friction. In the laboratory, a machine called a van de Graaff generator can be used to build up larger amounts of charge.

1. In the 1700s, all sorts of machines were made which built up large charges using the charging by friction method. See if you can find some pictures of these machines in your library.

Tumbling clothes

In a tumble drier, the clothes rub together as they go round and round. Answer these with your group:

2 Why do the hot clothes sometimes stick together when you take them out of a tumble drier?

3 When you pull the clothes apart, what do you hear?

4 What do you feel when you touch these clothes?

5 What happens to the hairs on your arm when the hot dry clothes are near? Try holding a rubbed balloon near your arm to see if this has any effect.

6 Sometimes, some of the clothes seem to push away from each other. Why do you think this happens? Try charging up two balloons and hanging them next to each other by threads. What happens when the places you rubbed are opposite each other?

7 If you take clothes out of the drier in the dark, what do you see?

More crackles and sparks

Sometimes when you pull off your jumper, you can hear crackles. If you do this in the dark, you may see sparks.

8 How do you think your clothes are getting charged?

In the picture on the right, Jason's feet are rubbing on the carpet.

9 What do you think happens as he walks down the stairs not touching the handrail?

10 What will happen if he touches the metal handrail?

Scientists think that electric sparks occur when charge escapes from one thing by jumping across a gap to another. When something loses its charge, they say that it is **discharged**. An object can be discharged by linking it to the ground by a metal wire or strip.

Lightning

Thunderstorms are sometimes called electric storms. They often occur in hot conditions when huge thunder clouds build up.

11 What do you think gets charged up in a thunderstorm?

12 Why do you hear thunder after you see the lightning?

Glenn lives on an island where they have never seen a thunderstorm.

13 Write a letter to Glenn explaining what you have found out about charges, crackles and sparks, and describing a thunderstorm.

14 How would you advise Glenn to keep safe in a thunderstorm.

D1.2 Charging up

Detecting charge

Kate found that when she rubbed a plastic comb with a cloth, it would pick up pieces of paper. Barry noticed that the comb attracted some of his hairs towards it after it had been rubbed. Barry reckoned that the more you rubbed the comb, the greater the number of paper pieces or hairs would be picked up. Kate disagreed. She said that only a bigger comb would pick up more paper or hair.

Investigate

Find out who was right, Kate or Barry. Then investigate the other materials in the table and find out which ones picked up the most charge when rubbed.

You need
Large and small plastic combs, scissors, paper, cloth, test materials.

Things to think about
- How can you tell which material has most charge on it?
- Does it matter how much you rub each item?
- Does charge leak away?
- How can you make your tests fair?
- How will you record your results?

What to do
- Plan your investigation.
- Ask your teacher to check your plan.
- Find out who was right, Kate or Barry.
- Compare the other materials.
- Make a table of your results to show which materials picked up most charge when rubbed.

Materials to test:

wood	glass
acetate	copper
iron	stone
china	brass
paper	plastic
polythene	rubber

Charge problems

1. When you unroll cling film, it often sticks to your hands. Why do you think this happens?
2. If you clean a dusty mirror with a dry duster, it can be even more dusty the next day. Why do you think this is so?

Two types of charge

Scientists have found that there are two types of electric charge. They call them **positive (+) charge** and **negative (−) charge**. If you rub a polythene rod, it becomes negatively charged. If you rub an acetate rod, it becomes positively charged.

Attraction and repulsion

Paul wondered why clothes from the tumble drier sometimes stuck together and sometimes pushed apart. He thought it would be possible to find out using charged polythene (−) and acetate (+) rods instead of clothes.

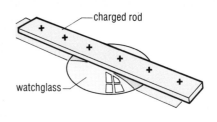

Investigate

Solve Paul's problem for him. Find out which sorts of charges **attract** (pull each other together) and which sorts **repel** (push each other apart).

You need
2 polythene rods, 2 acetate rods, cloth, items chosen by you.

Things to think about
* How can you balance a charged rod so that its ends move easily when another charged rod is brought near? The pictures may give you some ideas.
* How are you going to charge the rods?
* Will charge leak away if the rods rest on the bench?

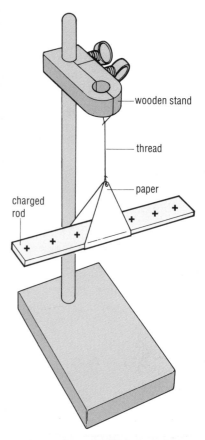

What to do
* Plan your investigation.
* Make a list of the equipment you will need.
* Ask your teacher to check your plan.
* Carry out your investigations.
* Record what you find.
* Copy and complete the following sentences:
   When positive charges are brought near each other, they . . .
   When negative charges are brought near each other, they . . .
   When a positive charge and a negative charge are brought near each other, they . . . .
* Decide whether each pair of items below will attract or repel:

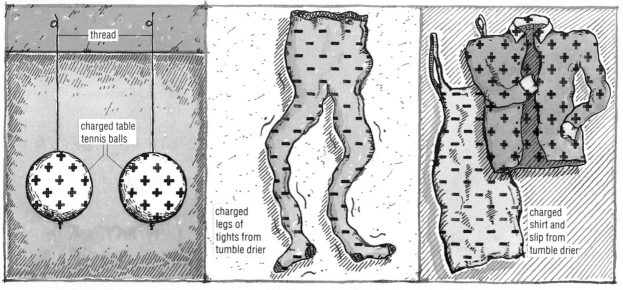

Lightning strikes 1900 – 1980	Mountain tops	Ridges	Valley sides	Valley bottoms	Woods	Lone trees
1900 – 1910	7	4	0	0	2	3
1911 – 1920	4	2	1	0	3	1
1921 – 1930	10	6	2	1	4	4
1931 – 1940	8	3	0	1	2	3
1941 – 1950	12	5	1	0	4	5
1951 – 1960	6	3	0	0	2	0
1961 – 1970	9	4	0	0	3	0
1971 – 1980	7	3	1	1	4	0

Charge jumps small gaps when you take off a jumper or empty a tumble drier. But when lightning strikes, charge jumps big gaps!

A survey was made of lightning strikes from 1900 to 1980 in the mountainous region of Cragland.

The picture shows Cragland as it was in 1920. Use the picture and the table of data to help you answer the following questions:

1 Altogether between 1900 and 1980:
How many strikes were there on mountain tops?
How many strikes were there on ridges?
How many strikes were there on valley sides?
How many strikes were there in valley bottoms?
How many strikes were there in woods?
How many strikes were there on lone trees?

2 Draw a bar chart to show the data in your answers above.

3 Which mountain would you expect to have the most lightning strikes?

4 Why do you think there were no lightning strikes on lone trees after 1950?

5 Where is the safest place to be in a thunderstorm in Cragland?

6 What safety rules can you think of for whenever you are in a thunderstorm?

7 Draw a safety poster for walkers in Cragland telling them what to do in a thunderstorm.

Did you know?

Dust and dirt particles in smoke from factory chimneys can cause serious pollution of the atmosphere. By using an **electrostatic dust precipitator** in the chimney the dust and dirt can be removed from the smoke. The dust sticks to charged plates inside the chimney.

A home '**ionizer**' can remove particles of dust from the air in a room. This can sometimes help people with asthma. The dust particles are attracted to a charged plate or wire.

Dusty records

Julie found that she had a problem keeping her LPs free of dust. If she carefully dusted them the dust seemed to come straight back again. This meant that the records didn't play properly. The stylus on her record player kept picking up dust. The sound was blurred and crackly, and sometimes the stylus stuck. Fiona used compact discs and did not have this problem.

Investigate

Design a way to keep Julie's records dust-free.

You need

Old record, items chosen by you.

Things to think about
- Why does the dust stick to the record?
- Can you make the dust stick to something else?
- How long do you need to keep the record free of dust?

What to do
- Plan your investigation.
- Make a list of the equipment you need.
- Ask your teacher to check your plan.
- Test your design. Does it work? If not, modify it.
- Design an advertisement for your record cleaner.
- Find out why Fiona does not get problems with the dust on her compact discs.

Electrostatic dust precipitators can help stop pollution like this

This ionizer will remove dust in the air

Dust on the record spoils the music

D2.1 Taking electricity with you

Every weekend, hundreds of people leave the safe world we know and lower themselves into the narrow, dark world underground. Imagine that you have suddenly found yourself in the middle of a deep, dark cave.

1 Make a list of the items which you would like to have with you.

2 If you could only have one item which would it be? Compare your ideas with other people's.

Lots of things need electricity to make them work. But they can't get their electricity from rubbed balloons and combs, or lightning sparks. It has to come from somewhere else. The pictures show some of the things that need electricity.

3 Choose *one* of the pictures and describe:
   what the item is
   what it is used for
   where it gets its electricity from.

4 Now do the same for the other pictures.

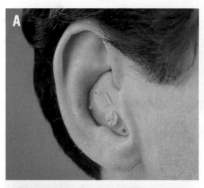

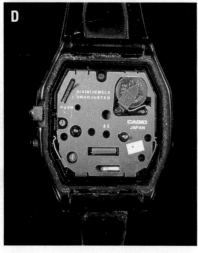

Battery survey

People often carry things around with them which need a supply of electricity. The electricity comes from **batteries**.

Investigate

In your class, carry out a survey of the different things people have at home which need batteries.

What to do
- Make a list of all the items you can think of which need batteries.
- Carry out your survey.
- Find out which is the most common item.
- Make a poster to show what you found in your survey.

The torch

Imagine that you have found an old torch in a cupboard. It looks in good condition but when you switch it on it does not work.

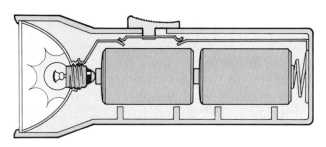

5 What would you do to make it work? Make a list of your ideas. Start with the first thing you would check and end with the last thing you would check.

6 Look at a real torch and find out how it works. You may be able to take the torch apart and see the smaller parts that are inside. If you do this, make a list of the parts and find out what they do.

7 Try to put the torch back together again!

Moved by batteries

Battery power can be used to move people and things about.

8 How is battery power helping the person in the picture?

9 List some more examples of battery power being used to move people and things about.

Electric delivery

Quickfood Ltd deliver sandwiches in petrol-driven vans. Their manager has read an article about electric-powered vans and is considering changing. Read the article on the right, then imagine that you are the manager of Quickfood.

10 Make a chart showing the good points and the bad points about electric vans. Discuss these with your group and see if you can add any more points.

11 Decide which type of vehicle you would want the company to buy.

12 Write a letter to your delivery drivers explaining your decision.

Electric delivery

Several companies in the area are considering changing to electric-powered vans for their delivery work. Electric vehicles are much slower than their petrol or diesel-powered counterparts. They are heavier, because of the batteries, and carry a smaller load as a result. But they are much quieter and they do not pollute the air with exhaust fumes. At present, electric vans are expensive to buy, but running costs are low, maintenance is easy and there are few working parts to go wrong. They do not have the range of petrol or diesel-powered vehicles and their batteries need lengthy recharging overnight. However, for local daytime delivery work, this is not normally a problem. Drivers find electric vans easy to drive because they have no starter, clutch or gears to worry about. But, without an engine to produce heat, the driving cab can be rather cold in the winter.

The materials used for making plugs and sockets have to be chosen very carefully. Some parts must let electricity flow through. Others must stop it flowing where it might be dangerous. But experiments with mains electricity can kill. What is needed is a safe way of testing materials to see which ones will let electricity flow through and which will not.

Test the material

A tool company is designing a new tool. It will be used near electrical wires, so the handle must be safe to hold even if the tool touches a bare wire.

Investigate

Find out which materials are safe to use for the handle of the tool.

You need
Battery, bulb and holder, test materials (see table), connecting wires and clips.

Useful information
- You can use the arrangement on the right to test different materials. The complete loop through battery, bulb, wires and test materials is called a **circuit**.
- The bulb will only light up if electricity can flow right round the circuit.
- Materials which let electricity flow through are called **conductors**. Materials which do not let electricity flow through are called **insulators**.

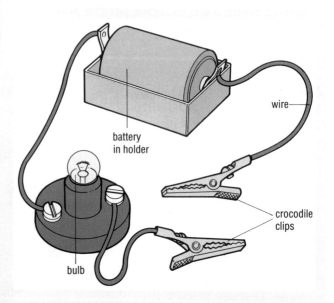

Things to think about
- How can you check that the circuit is working before you start testing any materials?
- How will you know whether the material you are testing is a conductor or an insulator?
- How will you record your results?

What to do
- Plan your investigation.
- Set up your test circuit and ask your teacher to check it.
- Test the different materials and record your findings.
- Which materials could be used for the handle?

Materials you can test:

nylon	wood
copper	aluminium
plastic	steel
rubber	glass
carbon	Perspex

Do liquids conduct electricity?

Investigate

Find out if liquids will let electricity flow through.

- Alter the circuit in your last investigation so that you can use it to test liquids. Test at least three liquids, but do not use any liquids that could catch fire. Do all the liquids give the same results?

Liquids you can test:

distilled water
salty water
dilute acid
lemon juice
copper sulphate solution

Warning! Acids are dangerous.
You must wear an apron and goggles when testing them.

An emergency light

Imagine that you are in an old, gloomy house. Night is approaching, the lights are not working and you do not have a candle or torch. However, in the house, you find some things which might be useful.

Investigate

Make an emergency light using the items in the picture.

Useful information
- Batteries have two connecting points, called **terminals**. Can you see what is written on a battery near each terminal?
- Electricity can only flow if there is a circuit with no gaps in it running from one terminal round to the other.

What to do
- Design your emergency light.
- Ask your teacher to check your design.
- Make your light and test it.
- Make a drawing of your design and label the parts.
- In what ways could your design be improved?

Current and voltage

The flow of electricity round a circuit is called a **current**. Scientists measure current in **amperes** (**A** for short), using a meter called an **ammeter**.

Batteries usually have a **voltage** marked on the side. The higher the voltage, the harder the battery pushes the current. Scientists measure voltage in **volts** (**V** for short) using a meter called a **voltmeter**.

Useful things found in the house

Did you know?

A battery pushes out electricity because of chemical reactions inside it. A single battery like the ones in a torch, watch or clock, is sometimes called an **electric cell**.

D2.3 Switches and circuits

One of the easiest ways of controlling electricity is to use a **switch**. With a switch, you can turn the flow of electricity on or off.

1 A torch has a switch in it. Make a list of all the things you can think of that are turned on and off using a switch.

Warning light

Mr Tomkins cannot hear door bells very well. He needs something to warn him when someone is at the door.

Investigate

Design a circuit so that, when a visitor presses a switch, a warning bulb lights up.

You need
Battery, wires, clips, light bulb, materials for making a switch (scissors, metal kitchen foil, card or wood, tape, paper clips)

Useful information
- A bulb will only light up if it is in a circuit with no gaps in it. If there is a gap in the circuit, then the bulb will be off.
- A switch is a handy way of opening and closing a gap in a circuit.

Things to think about
- You can see one type of switch in the picture on the right. What needs to happen so that electricity can flow through the switch?
- How will you make *your* switch?
- How will you connect it into your circuit?

What to do
- Design your door warning light.
- Ask your teacher to check your design.
- Make your warning light circuit and test it.
- Make a drawing of your design.
- Does it matter in which part of the circuit your switch is placed? Find out by changing its position.
- Describe any ways in which your design could be improved.

Switches

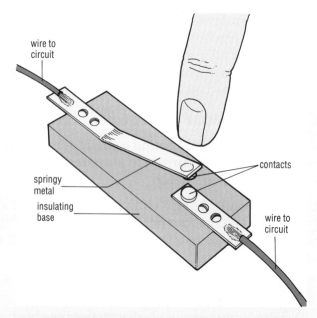

You can see what is happening in this switch. However, in most switches, the contacts are hidden away inside and moved by a lever, button or knob.

A light problem

Mr Tomkins has written a letter. He has another problem to be solved, and his friend has some ideas that need checking.

Investigate

Build the circuit designed by Mr Tomkins' friend. Find out the good and bad points about it.

You need
Battery, three bulbs, wires and clips, switch.

What to do
- Set up the circuit.
- Test the circuit to see if the bulbs shine.
- Investigate the circuit. See what happens when bulbs are taken out.
- Design and build a circuit with three bulbs in it.
- Write a letter to Mr Tomkins about your findings.

Bulbs in series

When bulbs are linked one after the other, scientists say they are in **series**. It's rather like a television series, where the programmes follow one after another. In a series circuit, the electricity flows through one bulb and then through the next, and so on. The bulbs were in series in the last warning light circuit you made.

2 What happens when one bulb is taken out of a series circuit?

3 What happens to the brightness as more bulbs are added to the circuit?

11, Draycott Road
Cleadon
Sunderland SR6 7TP

4th May 1990

Dear Headteacher,

I am writing to thank the students at your school who designed my clever warning light. It is now much easier for me to know when I have visitors, but there is a problem which I hope you can solve.

I need a warning circuit with two bulbs, so that I can have a light in the kitchen and one in the sitting room. A friend of mine has drawn a circuit that might work, but he has warned me that I would have problems if one bulb was broken or unscrewed.

Do you think the students could investigate this design for me and send me a report of their findings?

Yours sincerely,
Arthur Tomkins

P.S. Would it be possible to have three bulbs in the circuit so that I could have a bulb upstairs?

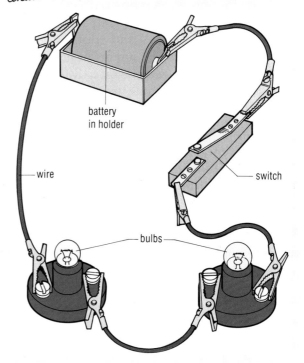

battery in holder

wire

switch

bulbs

Did you know?

In a bulb, only 10% of the electrical energy is changed to light. The rest is wasted as heat.

Test the circuits

Residents in Danger

People living in Tyneton are concerned about the large number of accidents in the village. Most of the problems happen after dark and scientists now think they know why. They blame the house lights. Apparently, if one bulb goes out all of the rest go out as well, and this causes accidents as people move around in the dark. Now, scientists have come up with a new circuit which they think may solve the problem. Soon, tests will start on the old and new circuits to see which works best.

Investigate

Test the circuits for the residents of Tyneton to find out which one solves their problem.

You need

Battery, 2 bulbs and bulb holders, switch, connecting wires and clips.

Useful information

- A **series** circuit gives the electricity only one path to travel along. If this path is blocked by a gap in the circuit, current can't flow.
- If the electricity is given a choice of paths, it can still flow even if one path is blocked. If a path was blocked on your way to school, you could still find another path and arrive on time! When bulbs are connected so that each is on a different path, scientists say that they are in **parallel**.

What to do

- Compare the circuits in the diagrams. What differences can you see between them?
- Build and test the first circuit (the **series** circuit).
- Record all your findings.
- Build and test the second circuit (the **parallel** circuit).
- Record all your findings.
- Write a newspaper article about your tests. Remember to say what differences you found between the series and parallel circuits.

Warning! Never attempt to investigate the mains electricity used in a house. Electrical equipment can kill.

How the lights should work

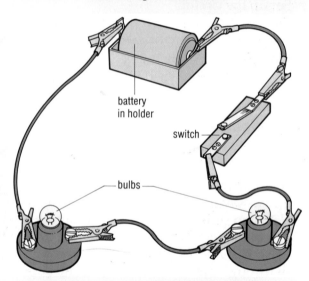

The bulbs in this circuit are in series

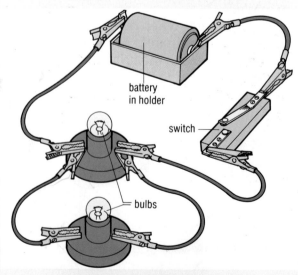

The bulbs in this circuit are in parallel

Illuminating model

Investigate

Make a model room with two working lights so that if one bulb is removed, the other stays lit.

You need
Battery, 2 bulbs and holders, 2 switches, wires and clips, cardboard, scissors, glue, sticky tape.

Things to think about
- What type of circuit do you need?
- Do you want both bulbs to be controlled by the same switch? Or do you want each bulb to be controlled by its own switch? It's your choice!

What to do
- Plan your model.
- Construct the model room.
- Make and fit the circuit.
- Test the circuit.

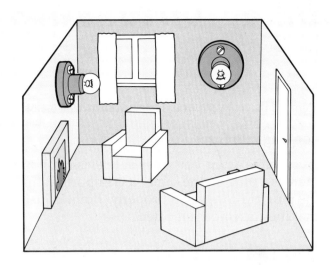

Alarming extras

Investigate

- You've made a model room with two lights. Now try adding a warning light which will come on if a burglar breaks in.

Extras you might need
Metal kitchen foil, bulb, holder, wire, clips.

Things to think about
- Where might a burglar enter the room?
- A switch turns things on by closing a gap in a circuit. Can you make a burglar close a gap in a circuit without knowing it? Would metal kitchen foil be useful?

Circuit symbols

Bulbs, batteries, switches and wires are often drawn as quick symbols. Use the symbols in the diagram to draw these circuits:
1. A circuit with a battery, a switch and two bulbs in series.
2. A circuit with a battery, a switch and two bulbs in parallel.

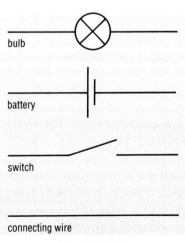

bulb

battery

switch

connecting wire

Circuit symbols

D2.5   Circuits and safety

Warning! Do not try any experiments at home with mains electricity.

Looking into fuses

If you have a new hair drier or television, you can't use it until there is a plug on the cable. It is important that the wires in the plug are connected properly. But it is just as important that the correct **fuse** is fitted.

Investigate

Find out how a fuse makes a circuit safer.

You need
Low voltage power supply, wires and clips, light bulb, thin fuse wire, thick fuse wire, heat proof mat, clothes pegs.

What to do
Warning! Do not touch the fuse wire when the power is switched on.
- Set up the circuit in the diagram.
- Test the circuit using thick fuse wire. Record anything you observe.
- Test the circuit using thin fuse wire. Record anything you observe.
- Was there any difference between the way the thick fuse wire behaved and the way the thin fuse wire behaved? Describe what you found.
- Make a poster about fuses. It should show what they do and why they are important.

Fuses at work

Electricity finds it more difficult to flow through some wires than others. Some wires have more **resistance** to the flow than others. When electricity passes through a wire, it produces heat. The more the wire resists the flow, the more heat is produced. Increasing the current also produces more heat. If the wire becomes too hot, it will burn up and break the circuit. Fuse wire works like this. If the current gets too high, the fuse wire melts and breaks the circuit before any other part can overheat. The fuse should always be the weakest part of the circuit. It needs to break before the rest of the circuit, but not too easily.

Fuses

low voltage power supply

wire

peg

fuse wire

heat proof mat

bulb

peg

1 In the fuses used in plugs, the fuse wire has a glass or china case around it. Why do you think this is?

The result of an electrical fault in a TV set

Did you know?

Every year, hundreds of people are killed or injured in fires caused by electrical faults. Many of these fires are caused by people fitting the wrong fuse. Some people have even put large nails across the gap meant for a fuse!

2 Why is this a very foolish thing to do?

3 In what other ways can electricity be dangerous?

Heating effects

The heat produced by an electric current can be put to good use. The equipment in the pictures gives off heat when electricity passes through a thin wire inside.

4 Can you think of any more examples of electricity being used to give heat? Make a list.

Kitchen hazards

Imagine you are the safety inspector checking a small hotel. You walk into the kitchen area and see the scene in the picture.

5 Write a letter to the kitchen staff pointing out the dangerous things you have found. In your letter, explain why these things are dangerous and what improvements should be made.

D3.1 Exploring with magnets

The walker in the picture is using a compass to help him find the way.

1 What else might he use?

2 Where does the compass point?

3 How can the compass help him if it gets foggy?

4 In case of bad weather conditions what other equipment should the walker have with him?

Compass

Did you know?

A compass needle is made of a **magnetic material**, usually steel. A magnetic material called **lodestone**, a type of iron ore, was discovered by the Greeks as long ago as 600 BC. Later in the Middle Ages sailors made compasses by using a piece of lodestone. They tied the lodestone to pieces of wood and floated it in a bowl of water.

Roderick does it again!

Roderick the famous racing pigeon has won yet again. This means he has brought his owner over a dozen trophies and cups during the past year.

Roderick has flown hundreds of miles and always arrived back in his loft ahead of his rivals. How does he do it?

Roderick's owner, Bert Parkin, attributes Roderick's success to a secret feed that keeps him in peak condition. This certainly helps Roderick to fly faster than his rivals but how does he find his way back to the loft? 'It's a mystery', admits his owner.

Now scientists may have found the answer. Tests on pigeons indicate that they may have magnetic material inside their heads. Could this be acting like a built in compass for racing pigeons? Early tests on racing pigeons show that this might be the case.

Racing pigeons

The newspaper article describes why a winning racing pigeon might be so successful.

5 What does his owner think makes him win?

6 How do scientists think racing pigeons might find their way back to their loft?

7 Can you think of any other animals or birds that travel over long distances and need to be able to find their way?

A problem with poles

Explorers find that compasses don't seem to work properly near the North and South Poles of the Earth. The pointing end of a compass needle tries to point *downwards* at the North Pole and *upwards* at the South Pole. Scientists think they can explain this. They say it's because the Earth behaves as though it has a bar magnet somewhere in the centre. But are their ideas right? Find out for yourself.

Investigate

Find out how a small plotting compass behaves near a bar magnet. Then make a model of the Earth with a bar magnet in the middle and find out whether it affects a plotting compass just like the real Earth does.

You need
Wooden clamp stand, bar magnet, plotting compass, thread, paper, globe paper lampshade.

What to do
- Hang the bar magnet in a paper cradle from the wooden clamp stand.
- Move the plotting compass around the magnet.
- Watch carefully what happens as the plotting compass is moved.
- Record what you see by drawing diagrams.
- Make a model Earth by suspending the bar magnet in the centre of the paper lampshade.
- Move the plotting compass round the outside of your model Earth.
- Remembering what the explorers found near the North and South Poles, mark on your lampshade where you think the poles are on your model Earth.
- Draw a poster of your model. Describe how the model works.
- Compare your poster with those from other groups.

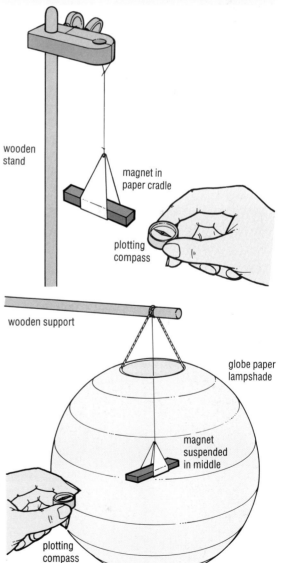

wooden stand

magnet in paper cradle

plotting compass

wooden support

globe paper lampshade

magnet suspended in middle

plotting compass

D3.2   Investigating magnets

Comparing magnetic forces

Rachel noticed that some magnets would pick up longer chains of pins than others. David found that it was harder to pull some magnets off the steel base of a clamp than others.

Investigate

Design and carry out an experiment to compare the forces from different magnets.

You need
2 different bar magnets, items chosen by you.

Things to think about
* How are you going to tell which magnet pulls most?
* How are you going to make your test fair?

What to do
* Plan your experiment.
* Make a list of the items you need.
* Check your plan with your teacher.
* Carry out your experiment and record your results.
* Which magnet gives the biggest force?

What materials are attracted to magnets?

Magnets attract some things but not others. Materials which are attracted to a magnet are called magnetic materials. Materials *not* attracted to a magnet are called non-magnetic materials.

Investigate

Find out what materials are attracted to a magnet.

You need
Magnet, materials to test (see table).

What to do
* Test as many materials as possible.
* Make a table showing which materials are attracted to a magnet and which are not.

Materials you can test:

glass	aluminium	steel
wood	plastic	polythene
copper	nickel	brass
iron	cobalt	acetate

Did you know?

Strong magnets can affect digital watches.

Magnets should never be brought close to a colour television screen. They can distort the colours in the picture.

Fields and poles

Every magnet has a **magnetic field** around it. This is the space where the magnetic forces do their pushing and pulling. The field seems to be concentrated at points called **poles**. You can see the field by sprinkling iron filings onto paper which is resting on the magnet. And you can **map** the field more accurately using a plotting compass.

Investigate

Use a plotting compass to make a map of the field round a bar magnet. Use your map to decide where the poles of the magnet are.

You need
Bar magnet, plotting compass, paper.

Useful information
Plotting compasses can show you part of a magnetic field. The line running through the compasses in the diagram is called a **magnetic field line**. By drawing enough magnetic field lines, you can map the whole field.

Things to think about
- How can you use just one plotting compass to draw a map with lots of field lines?
- How can you work out where the poles of the magnet are?

What to do
- Plan your experiment.
- Map the magnetic field.
- The Earth behaves like a big magnet. Use your plotting compass to map the Earth's magnetic field in your school field or playground.

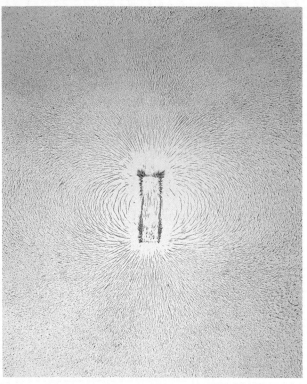

Using iron filings to show a magnetic field

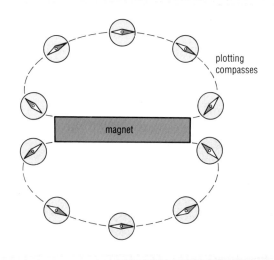

Using plotting compasses to show magnetic field lines

Pole pushes and pulls

Scientists have found that every magnet has two poles, a **north-seeking** pole and a **south-seeking** pole. They usually call them **north** and **south** poles, or **N** and **S** for short. If a magnet is hung up, it tries to point so that its north-seeking pole is towards the North Pole of the Earth.

Investigate

- Find out what happens when you arrange two bar magnets with their poles near each other as in the diagram.
- Work out some rules to describe what you see.

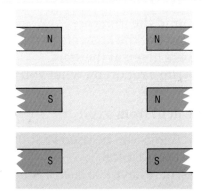

D3.3   Electromagnets

In the picture, a giant **electromagnet** is being used to lift things in a scrapyard. The electromagnet is a huge **coil** of wire wound round an iron **core**. It becomes a powerful magnet when an electric current is switched on and flows through the coil. The block is released when the current is switched off.

Making an electromagnet

Investigate

Design and make a small electromagnet for lifting pins. Then find out the answers to the following questions:

- How many ways can you make an electromagnet give a stronger pull?
- What is the effect of using a steel core instead of an iron core?
- Why would a steel core be no good in a scrapyard?

You need
Power supply or batteries, wires and clips, pins, switch, items in the diagram, items chosen by you.

Things to think about
- How are you going to switch the current on and off?
- Will you need to change the voltage?
- How will you be able to tell if the electromagnet is giving a stronger force?
- What will you need to record?
- How can you make sure your tests are fair?

What to do
- Plan your circuit.
- Check your plan with your teacher.
- Make your electromagnet by winding wire round the iron core.
- Find out the answers to the questions you were given at the start.
- Write a report on what you found.

The field from a coil

Iron filings can be used to show the magnetic field round a coil.

1 Where have you seen a similar field pattern?

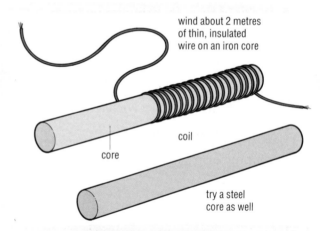

wind about 2 metres of thin, insulated wire on an iron core

coil

core

try a steel core as well

Making an electromagnet

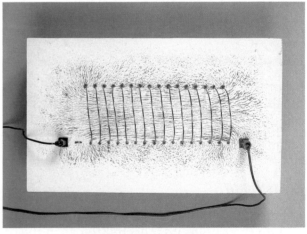

Showing the field round a coil

Electromagnets under test

Two electromagnets have the same sized iron core, but each has a different number of turns in the coil. The table shows the results of dipping the two electromagnets into a boxful of pins. Each electromagnet was tested eight times, with the current set to a different value each time.

2 Which coil picked up the most pins when the current was 1 A? Was it the 10 turn coil or the 30 turn coil?

3 Was this true for all the other current settings?

4 Plot a graph to show how many pins were picked up by the 10 turn coil at each current setting.

5 Plot a graph to show how many pins were picked up by the 30 turn coil at each current setting.

6 What do the shapes of the graphs tell you about the electromagnets?

7 It costs more to use a larger current. Why is there no point in using the 30 turn coil on the 4 A current setting?

8 You need to divide 1000 pins into boxes holding approximately 20 pins each. You want to do the job as quickly as possible. And you want to use as little current as possible. Which electromagnet would you use and at which current setting?

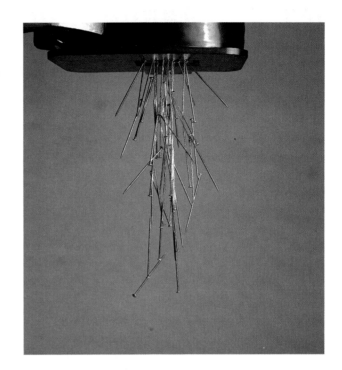

| Current in | Pins picked up | |
amperes (A)	10 turn coil	30 turn coil
0.5	2	6
1.0	4	12
1.5	10	30
2.0	17	50
2.5	22	67
3.0	28	68
3.5	33	68
4.0	38	68

Magnetic relays

Electromagnets can be used for switching. With a **magnetic relay**, a circuit with thin wires and a tiny switch can be used to switch on a big, powerful circuit. In many cars, relays are used for switching on the headlights, the horn and the heated rear window.

Look at the diagram of the magnetic relay:

9 What happens to the electromagnet when the switch is closed?

10 What effect does this have on the iron lever?

11 What does the iron lever do to the two contacts?

12 What effect does this have on the bulb?

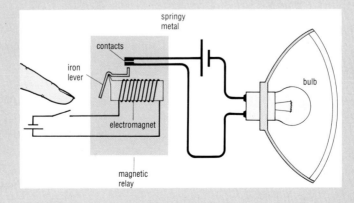

Using a magnetic relay to control a bulb

Separating mixtures

Magnetic materials can be removed from mixtures of substances by using magnets or electromagnets.

Investigate

■ Use a magnet to separate the magnetic materials from a mixture.

You need
Magnet, paper, mixture of materials.

Things to think about
- How can you make sure that you have removed every bit of magnetic material?
- How can you make sure that the magnetic materials don't stay stuck to the magnet?

Measuring thickness

In a car factory new cars are given several coats of paint. The paint thickness is checked with a thickness gauge using an electromagnet. When the paint is too thin it is harder to pull the magnet off the car than when the paint is the correct thickness.

1 Why is it important to get the paint thickness correct?

2 Why can't the thickness be measured with a ruler?

Investigate

Use a magnet to find out how thick a piece of card is compared with a sheet of paper.

You need
Magnet, paper, scissors, newtonmeter, card to test, sticky tape, string.

Things to think about
- Will it be easier to pull the magnet off the steel base of the clamp stand if there is paper between the magnet and the base?
- Will the force needed depend on the number of sheets of paper between the magnet and the base?
- How can you measure the force?
- How can you use your results to compare the card with the sheets of paper?

Separating metals in a scrapyard

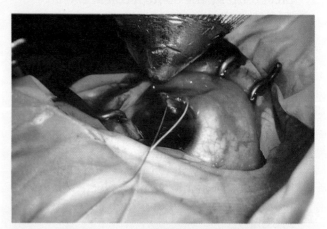

Removing a metal fragment from an eye

Checking the paint thickness on a car body

What to do
- Plan your investigation.
- Do your experiment.
- Find out how many sheets of paper make the same thickness as the piece of card.
- Make a leaflet describing how your method works.

A smooth ride

The picture shows a special train called **Maglev** which runs at Birmingham airport. When it is running, electromagnets keep the train 15 mm above the track. A computer controls the current going to the electromagnets so that the train stays the same height above the track at all times. This gives a very smooth friction-free ride as the train is not in contact with the rails. The train is powered by a special motor using both electricity and magnetism.

3 Draw a poster advertising the advantages of Maglev.
4 Why do you think all our trains are not being changed to be like Maglev?
5 In the winter, when it is icy, some trains cannot run. Maglev keeps going! Why do think this is so?

Maglev

Magnetism in the home

Magnets have many different uses in the home. Two examples are door catches and can openers. Loudspeakers have magnets in them. So does any equipment with an electric motor in it.

These use magnets or electromagnets

6 Make a survey of all the things in your home that use magnets or electromagnets to make them work.
7 Imagine how life at home would be changed if there were no magnets. Write a story about what would happen if you woke up one morning and found that no magnets or electromagnets worked any more.

Did you know?

Door chimes have an electromagnet in them. When the electromagnet is switched on, it pulls an iron rod across to hit one chime. When the electromagnet is switched off, the rod springs back to hit the other chime. This gives the 'bing bong' sound.

8 What switches the electromagnet on, then off?

Electric bells have an electromagnet in them. The electromagnet is switched on and off automatically, very fast. Each time it switches on, it pulls a tiny hammer across to hit the bell.

9 Set up an electric bell in the classroom. See if you can find out how the electromagnet switches itself on and off automatically.

Investigate

Use your scientific skills to solve the following problems.

With each one, remember to:
- plan your work carefully.
- check your plans with your teacher.
- record any findings you make.

You need

Materials shown in the diagrams, glue, scissors, sticky tape.

Model lighthouse

Build a model lighthouse with a bulb that lights.

Things to think about
- What circuit will you use to make the bulb light?
- How will the lighthouse be constructed?
- Could you make the light flash on and off?

What to do
- Design and build your model.
- Test the model.
- Imagine that the lighthouse is going to be sold as a kit in toy shops. Design a set of instructions so that other people can make your model. Draw a poster to advertise it.

Things you might need to make a model lighthouse

Electric fruit

Make a battery by putting a copper plate and a zinc plate into a lemon. Find out which fruits make the best batteries!

Things to think about
- How are you going to tell which fruits work best?

What to do
- Set up a battery using a lemon.
- Test your battery.
- Make batteries using other fruits and test them.
- Which fruits worked best? Prepare a report of your findings. It could be an article or a talk to the rest of your class.
- Most people use ordinary batteries rather than batteries made of fruit. Why do you think this is?

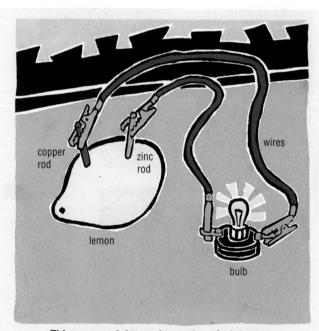

Things you might need to make a fruit battery

Hand steady game

Make a hand steady game to test how carefully people can move a loop along a wire without touching the wire.

Things to think about

- Will a bulb light up if there are gaps in the circuit?
- Should the bulb be off if the loop isn't touching the wire?
- How can you make the bulb come on if the loop touches the wire?
- Will you use a conductor or an insulator for the wire and the loop?
- What shape will you make the wire?

What to do

- Design and build the circuit.
- Test your game.
- Some scientists think that people can concentrate better in quiet rooms. How could you use your hand steady game to find out if this evidence is correct? Try it!

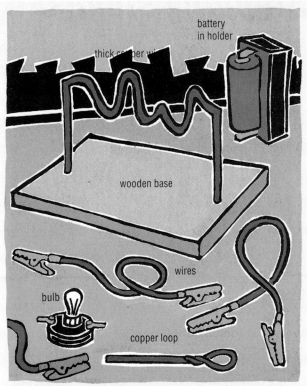

Things you might need to make a hand-steady game

Quiz board

Build a quiz board that makes a bulb shine when a correct answer is given.

Useful information

- People could choose questions and answers by attaching clips to the sides of a card.
- You could fix strips of metal kitchen foil behind the card so that each starts by a question and ends by the correct answer.
- To make the bulb light up, there has to be an unbroken circuit through the battery, the bulb and any one of the foil strips.

Things to think about

- What five questions will you ask about electricity and magnets?
- In what order will you list the questions on the card? In what order will you list the answers? The quiz will be too easy if the two orders are the same!
- How will you fix the foil strips across the back of the card?
- Why is it important that the foil strips don't touch each other? How can you make sure that they don't?

Things you might need to make a quiz board

What to do

- Design and build your circuit.
- Think up five questions (and answers) on electricity and magnets.
- Test your board on the people in another group.

Stepping stones

Bright sparks

1. Read the information below about electrical storms.
2. Make a list of the ten most important words.
3. Close the book so that you cannot see the information any more. Use your list of ten words to help you prepare a report about lightning and thunderclouds.

Scientists believe that electrical storms are caused by water droplets which collide inside thunderclouds. Large drops of water become positively charged, but the air around them gains a negative charge. The drops fall and rise until the charge becomes so big inside the cloud that it is like a giant electricity store. After about 15 minutes the lightning flash occurs.

It has been estimated that there are approximately 16 million thunderstorms per year in the world. 1800 are taking place at any one time. Despite the enormous power of lightning, less than twenty people are killed in Britain each year by lightning strikes.

Circuit puzzle

Copy and complete the crossword.

Across
1. We get this from electricity.
2. This protects a circuit.
3. The flat end of a torch battery.
4. Unit of electrical 'push'.

Down
1. Another name for plus.

Put it right!

Some of the words in the paragraph below are wrong.
4. Make a list of the words that are wrong.
5. Next to the list, make a list of the words that they should be.

When a dome is connected to a battery, electricity flows through the dome and makes it shine. The path through the dome, wires and battery is called a circle. There are two ways in which extra domes can be added to a circle. One is to connect the domes in a row so that current flows through one then the other. We say the domes are connected in stereo. The other method is to connect the domes side by side so that each has its own branch of the circle. We say these domes are connected in parasite. If one dome is removed from three domes in stereo the other two domes will go out. If one dome is removed from three domes in parasite the other two domes remain lit. Appliances used in the home are always connected in parasite so that they can be switched on and off without affecting any other appliance.

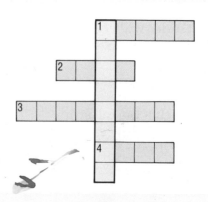

Magnetic gaps

6 Copy out the following paragraph and complete it by choosing words to go in the blanks.

The magnetic force from a magnet seems to come from two points near its ends. These are called the _____ _____ and the _____ _____ of the magnet. If you hang a magnet up from a piece of cotton, it will try to turn so that its _____ _____ points north. A _____ has a tiny magnet in it which points north.

Materials which are attracted to magnets are called _____ materials; _____ and _____ are two examples. Many materials are not attracted to magnets, including _____ and _____ .

There is one type of magnet which can be switched on and off. It is called an _____ . It has a _____ in the middle, which is often made of _____ . Around this, there is a _____ of wire. It only gives a magnetic pull if _____ is flowing through.

Coil count

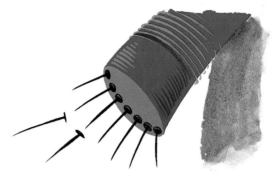

Here are the results of an experiment to see the effect of increasing the number of turns on the coil of an electromagnet. The electromagnet was tested by hanging as many nails as possible from it end to end. The same current was passed through each time.

Number of turns	10	20	30	40	50	60	70	80	90	100
Number of nails	1	1	1	2	3	4	4	6	7	8

7 Draw a bar chart to show these results.
8 Describe what happens when the number of turns on an electromagnet is increased.
9 Explain why the number of nails sometimes stays the same, even though more turns have been added.

Fast food

Dinner table railway

'The meal now standing at platform . . .'. Things never quite went this far in the home of the Frenchman Gaston Menier in the 1880s. Nevertheless, dinner was a strange and wonderful affair. Meals were brought straight from the kitchen to the table by an electric railway. Carriages bearing the food ran on a four-rail track and were controlled by the host. No servants were needed, nor did guests have to pass the dishes from hand to hand. The train could carry 20 kg of food at up to 2 mph. It gave the meal 'particular liveliness and intimacy', said one guest.

This is an article from an old newspaper. It describes a very strange use for electrical circuits.

10 Describe what you think meal time would be like if you lived in a house that served food by electric railway.
11 What other uses could you find for an electric railway in a house?
12 Design a circuit that could be used to let the people eating tell the people in the kitchen that they were ready for more food.

Index

Acknowledgements

The illustrations are by: **Brian Beckett, Ed Carr, Lynn Chadwick, Nick Duffy, Nick Hawken, David Holmes, Stephen Holmes, Mark Oliver, Lynne Riding, Mark Rogerson, Mike Sharp** and **Tony Simpson.**

The publishers would like to thank the following for supplying photos:
Allied Bakeries 45 (top right); **Allsport** 72 (right, middle row); **Amey Roadstone Company** 69 (centre, top); **Heather Angel** 12 (top right); **Ark Communications** 83; **Banbury Homes & Gardens /The Public Relations Business** 74 (left); **BIP Chemicals** 74 (centre); **Birmingham International Airport** 121 (top); **Black & Decker** 76 (A); **Boots** 38 (top right), 45 (left, bottom row); **Boxmag-Rapid** 118 (top); **Braun Electric** 113 (left); **Britvic Soft Drinks** 45 (far right, second row); **Butter Information Council** 45 (top left); **J. Allan Cash** 18 (left), 69 (top left and right), 86 (top); **Bruce Coleman/Mark Boulton** 13 (left), 14 (right, bottom row), /**Jane Burton** 9, 10 (left), 12 (bottom right), 14 (top and second row, middle bottom row), 28 (bottom centre), 29 (bottom right), /**Alain Compost** 12 (bottom left), 29 (bottom centre), 87, /**Inigo Everson** 29 (bottom left), /**Al Giddings** 29 (top left), /**Gordon Langsbury** 29 (top left), /**Leonard Lee Rue III** 29 (top centre), /**L.C. Marigo** 13 (right), /**Prato** 28 (top left), /**Hans Reinhard** 28 (top right and bottom right), 72 (left, top row), 81 (top), /**H. Rivarola** 21, /**Norbert Rosing** 12 (top left), /**John Shaw** 10 (right), /**Werner Stoy** 76 (H), /**Kim Taylor** 11, 14 (third row), /**Gunter Ziesler** 10 (centre); **Fiona Corbridge** 76 (C), 78 (bottom right), 85 (left), 89, 114 (top left); **Cull Photographic** 38 (top left and bottom right), 45 (left, second row; centre and right, third row; centre, bottom row), 50, 51 (top), 53 (bottom), 70, 76, (F and G), 79, 80, 81 (bottom), 85 (right), 88, 93 (top), 104 (bottom row), 106, 108, 121 (centre and top right, bottom row); **Electricity Council** 105 (bottom); **Electrolux** 93 (bottom right); **Flour Advisory Bureau** 38 (centre left and right), 43; **Peter Gould** 72 (bottom row), 78 (top left and right), 98 (bottom), 116, 117, 118 (bottom), 119; **Sally and Richard Greenhill** 18 (top and bottom right); **Holt Studios** 28 (top centre), 53 (top); **Eric and David Hosking** 17 (top), 54; **The Hutchison Library** 68 (right, bottom row); **Institute of Hydrology** 86 (bottom); **Jacob's Bakery** 45 (centre, second row); **Kenwood** 121 (right, bottom row); **Frank Lane Agency** 114 (bottom); **London Fire Brigade** 112; **Lyons Maid** 76 (B); **Mattessons Wall's** 45 (left, third row); **Miele** 99 (top); **Moët & Chandon** 45 (right, second row); **Moorfields Eye Hospital** 120 (centre); **Mountain Breeze** 103 (bottom); **National Dairy Council** 38 (bottom left), 49 (bottom); **Nutbourne Manor** 41 (bottom); **Oldham Crompton Batteries** 104 (centre, middle row); **Alan Owens** 19, 74 (right), 76 (D), 93 (middle and bottom left), 98 (top); **Oxford Scientific Films** /**John Cooke** 14 (left, bottom row), /**Pam & Willy Kemp** 16, /**Michael Leach** 76 (E), /**(London Scientific Films** 49 (top); **Peugeot Cycles** /**Summerfield Morgenthau** 72 (centre, middle row); **Philips** 104 (right, middle row), 121 (below right, bottom row); **Prestige/Paragon Communications** 121 (left, bottom row); **Rentokil Group** 59; **Rockwool** 69 (bottom right); **Science Photo Library/Alex Bartel** 120 (top), /**A.B. Dowsett** 51 (bottom), /**Graham Evans** 17 (bottom), /**Simon Frazer** 103 (top), /**John Giannicchi** 22 (bottom), /**Nelson Medina** 99 (bottom), /**National Institute of Allergy and Infectious Diseases** 61 (top), /**Dr K. Roberts, John Innes Institute** 39, 41 (top), /**Jonathan Watts** 61 (bottom); **Shell** 92; **Silva (UK)** 114 (top right); **Smiths Crisps** 45 (right, bottom row); **Spanish Tourist Office** 68 (left, bottom row); **Starkey Laboratories** 104 (left, middle row); **St. Ivel** 44; **Swan Housewares** 113 (right); **Swed-logs** 68 (right, middle row); **Twins and Multiple Births Association** 22 (top); **T.P. Activity Toys** 72 (right, top row); **Vauxhall Motors** 120 (bottom); **Vessa /G.W. Associates** 105 (top); **Anthony Waltham** 104 (top row); **Warner Howard/PL Communications** 77; **Wimpey** 68 (top), 69 (bottom left); **Zefa** 28 (bottom left), 68 (left, middle row), 71, 72 (centre, top row and left, middle row), 110, 115.

The publishers would like to thank **Alexandra Junior School**, the CDT department at **Sydenham School**, and the **Twins and Multiple Births Association** for their help.

The **Twins and Multiple Births Association** can be contacted at 51 Thicknall Drive, Pedmore, Stourbridge, West Midlands DY9 0YH.

Oxford University Press
Walton Street
Oxford OX2 6DP

Oxford New York Toronto
Delhi Bombay Calcutta Madras Karachi
Kuala Lumpur Singapore Hong Kong Tokyo
Nairobi Dar es Salaam Cape Town
Melbourne Auckland Madrid
and associated companies in
Berlin Ibadan

ISBN 0 19 914 325 0

Typeset by Pentacor PLC, High Wycombe, Bucks
Printed in Belgium